Gardening with Conscience

Gardening with Conscience

The Organic-Intensive Method

Marny Smith

—— *Illustrated by Frances Boynton* ——

—— A Vineyard Book ——
The Seabury Press / New York

For Helen and Fred

1981
The Seabury Press, Inc.
815 Second Avenue
New York, N.Y. 10017

Printed in the United States of America

Library of Congress Catalog in Publication Data

Smith, Marny.
  Gardening with conscience.
  Bibliography: p. 85
  1. Vegetable gardening.   2. Organic gardening.
I. Title.   II. Title: Organic-intensive method.
SB324.3.S63   635'.0484   81-4886
ISBN 0-8164-2325-3   AACR2

Contents

v

Introduction
by Joan Dye Gussow

You are about to begin a wonderful book—with a wonderful goal—to help you increase your food self-sufficiency. But it would be best not to think of it that way to start with. It would be best to start by thinking small—as Marny Smith suggests—by looking around your yard to see whether there isn't some spot which gets at least six hours of sunshine a day. Perhaps a lawn you are tired of seeding, feeding, weeding, and mowing year after year.

We had to cut down a huge oak tree to get our sunshine, and it wasn't an easy decision. The man who came to take it down (people who cut down trees are heartless brutes, right? Wrong.) kept commenting on the loss. "There's nothing wrong with this tree," he kept saying as he stood in his little container atop his cherry-picker crane. "It's a shame to cut it down." I was so upset I had to go inside.

I tell this story to assure you that Marny Smith is right when she insists that you have to have six hours of sunshine—or more. Now many authors would tell you that you needed six hours of sunshine and leave it at that. This author doesn't do that. This author tells you how to figure where the sun will fall in the summer, if you're thinking about your garden in the winter.

There is a nice, sensible person writing this book, a person who has dug and planted many vegetable gardens and who, in telling you what she has done, makes it seem quite probable that you should do it too. "Since my preferred time to begin a garden is in the fall . . . I will proceed as if that is the time you have chosen to begin. You have sent off your soil sample to be tested." (Don't panic. She's already told you how to do that) ". . . and now, while you are waiting for the results, is the perfect time to begin building your compost piles." Just like that.

She leads you, step by step, through the process of planning a garden and on, step by step, through the things one does to actually *make* a garden. The book is wonderfully organized (with a full stress on both of those words) and I suspect its author is too. Just about the time you think "but she hasn't told me about *that*," she does. Or she tells you that she'll tell you later, "There are ways to make a little (water) go a long ways which I describe in a later chapter on 'Garden Maintenance.' " And the lady (in this case I use the term as a compliment) who has written this book is also a realist. If you *must* start your garden in the spring—the time most people remember that they want to start a garden—you can even use a little commercial fertilizer—just this once!!

My husband read part of the manuscript and commented that the book might have been called "gardening with consciousness" because he felt that the effect of her very explicit instructions about how to decide whether your land had the right slope and the right sun exposure (and what to do if it didn't) would be to make people much more aware of their own surroundings. What kinds of organic materials are around my house, my neighborhood? What are those weeds, and what are they telling me? What kind of soil do I have? Are those insects friendly?

Of course I don't agree with her about everything. She likes wider paths (we're space hoarders—after all we had to cut down an oak tree to get the space) and we plant carrots all over the bed rather than in mini rows, and we plant broccoli and other large plants in a diamond pattern and we *always* mulch our beds in the winter since we decided it keeps the soil in better condition, and we double dig *every* time we plant because we have a heavy clay soil. But Marny Smith wouldn't expect everyone to do everything any one way. For it is clear that she knows—as does anyone who gardens—that food growing is an art. One learns only over time just what to do and when to do it in any given year on your particular piece of land with your particular microclimate (whether "it" is digging, mulching, planting, or pulling). What is wonderful about this book is that, recognizing that food growing is an art, it doesn't start by assuming you are an artist—it tells you how to become one.

I

1

Why Grow a Vegetable Garden?

Between five and six on most afternoons from April to November, I head for the garden with my basket to pick our supper. Immediately, I stave off hunger with a random selection of snacks—crisp green beans, a tart roquette leaf or two, or perhaps a handful of raspberries, air-cleaned and sun-ripened. In April I fill my basket with fresh radishes, lettuces, and arucola combined with spinach that has wintered over in the garden. May offers versatile snow peas, scallions, and young kohlrabi to be eaten raw in salads or stir-fried in the wok. June marks the beginning of the bean parade, which lasts most of the summer, and the first cucumbers, squashes, and various members of the cabbage family. When at last the familiar favorites—tomatoes, potatoes, peppers, and eggplant—ripen, our garden becomes an embarrassment of choices.

The exquisite taste of a tomato warm from the afternoon sun

or the sweet crunch of a Sugar Snap pea picked and eaten on the spot; summer squash picked at six and lightly steamed for dinner at seven, or fresh beet greens simmered gently in their own juices; baby Brussels sprouts sweetened by frost, or all the asparagus you can eat—these are samples of the pleasures in store for you when you have a vegetable garden. To compare the sweetness of an ear of corn, popped into boiling water and eaten moments after being plucked from its mother stalk, with an ear that has spent forty-eight hours in a crate on a truck before being wrapped in plastic is to liken freshly baked bread to a stale cracker. The taste of a new potato, freshly dug, is like no potato you've ever tasted before. Experiencing any or all of these gustatory treats will convince you that home-grown vegetables taste better!

I saw a small sign standing among flowers in a garden once and was struck by its words:

> The kiss of the sun for pardon
> The song of the birds for mirth
> One is nearer God's heart in a garden
> Than anywhere else on earth.

I truly feel "nearer God's heart" as I work with the earth, seeds, and the plants they yield. We all seem to be working together—nature, God, and I—doing our share to make things grow.

I feel nearer God's heart for other reasons, too. When my conscience pricks me with the knowledge that so many in the world are hungry, I know that having a garden means that our family is not draining the world food supply as much as we once were, because we eat more vegetable meals and less meat. Nor are we using as much nonrenewable energy. Petroleum products are used in every step of commercial food production from growing through processing, packaging, refrigerating, freezing, trucking, and displaying in the market. In New England 80 percent of the food eaten comes from outside the region, and much of the fresh produce comes from as far away as California. Besides the fact that California soils are developing problems that may diminish their food growing capacity, it takes a lot of petroleum-based fuel to get that food from farm to table, while very little *human* energy brings food to the dinner table from the backyard garden.

Our vegetable garden has saved us money because we are not paying for the processing and transporting. During a six-month period from May to October, 1979, I kept a careful record of vegetable production in a garden only slightly larger than a single car garage, calculating its value in supermarket prices, and found that we had saved over $320. Thus a pleasant and healthy investment of time and energy paid off in consistent savings. I can think of no other hobby that increases the family income in goods rather than depleting it!

My own backyard garden, which is about the size of a two and a half car garage, is just large enough to provide our food almost year round—for an average four people in residence—and at the same time give me good exercise. Aside from the initial breaking of the ground, which can be strenuous, gardening is a simple exercise, a kind of slow stretching of muscles that is suitable at any age, eight to eighty. Any fatigue felt afterward is combined with a sense of accomplishment.

2

The Organic-Intensive Method: What Is It and Why Use It?

The first tenet of gardening organically is FEED THE SOIL, NOT THE PLANT. The second is PUT BACK MORE THAN YOU TAKE OUT. The method I use is built on these two tenets and can best be described as organic/intensive.

"Organic," quite simply, means using only materials in their natural state, as opposed to using chemical fertilizers. Plants are fed a rich compost of these materials—tree leaves, plant residues, fruit and vegetable wastes, manures and wood ashes, all partially decomposed into humus—rather than a quick fix of chemical formulas.

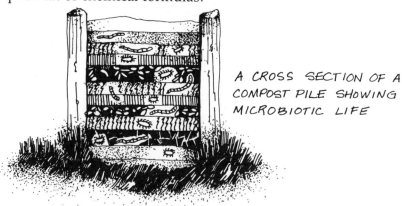

A CROSS SECTION OF A COMPOST PILE SHOWING MICROBIOTIC LIFE

Commercially prepared fertilizers contain chemicals in an ionized form that plants can use immediately. They are only available to the plants for a short time, however, and must be applied repeatedly to maintain a high level of growth. Organic gardeners, on the other hand, rely on soil microbes to digest organic matter, thereby converting elements into ions that are available to plants. Microbes do this at a slow steady pace over a long period of time, or as long as there is plenty of organic matter in the soil. This microbiotic life is essential to a rich, healthy soil, and will eventually disappear if chemical fertilizers are used and no organic matter is added. This is what farmers mean when they refer to soil as exhausted or "dying."

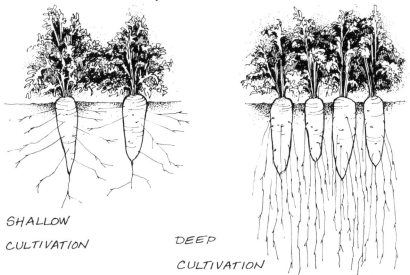

SHALLOW
CULTIVATION

DEEP
CULTIVATION

The "intensive" part of the term organic/intensive refers to the closer spacing of the plants made possible by extra deep cultivation. Rather than spreading out near the ground surface, the plants' roots go down through the loosened soil looking for nourishment. Intensive also refers to the continual use of all cultivated garden space through crop succession, overlapping, and catch-cropping, which I'll explain later. No empty spaces mean higher productivity.

Besides producing succulent vegetables, this method is highly appropriate to the 1980s when energy is short and recycling is returning as part of our way of life. Anyone can do it almost anywhere. I remember my frustration at being told several years ago that our tired lawn was too tough for a roto-tiller and we would need a tractor to turn it into a garden. Later I learned that the best gardens are carefully dug by hand, and fertilized through composting and mulching with recycled waste materials.

Disposing of garbage in ways that are economical and environmentally sound will continue to pose serious challenges to public works departments throughout the 1980s. Reducing the stream of waste by recycling some of it right in the backyard—the newspapers, food wastes, wood ashes, and leaves—can lower the cost of coping with this nationwide problem.

Gardening organically without commercially prepared chemical fertilizers and pesticides keeps the soil healthy. In the same manner, reducing our intake of additives, preservatives, and pesticide residues is a form of preventive medicine. Both human bodies and soil in a healthy condition will resist disease better than bodies or soil weakened by poor nutrition. Although food scientists and horticulturists today argue that there is no definite scientific proof that food grown organically is more nutritious, Sir Albert Howard wrote about the connection between soil health and human health thirty-odd years ago, in his book *Soil and Health*. Based on testimony gathered from people all over the world, Howard concluded that recycling plant and animal wastes through composting to restore garden soil fertility year after year was directly responsible for the unusual good health of all his respondents. He even went so far as to say that "soil fertility is the basis of the public health system of the future (p. 189)."

In the years ahead, space for doing anything will be increasingly limited. Abraham Lincoln foresaw this over 100 years ago when he predicted that "Population (will) increase rapidly, more rapidly than in former times, and ere long the most valuable of all arts will be the art of deriving a comfortable subsistence from the smallest area of soil." One of the great assets of an organic/intensive garden is that it can be tucked into a very small corner and still produce prolifically. I harvested 420 pounds in seven months from the single-car-

garage sized garden I mentioned earlier. Instead of a tradition-
ally conceived large rectangular garden, cultivated and planted
in rows one to two feet apart, an organic/intensive garden consists of beds four to five feet wide and up to twenty-five feet
long in any arrangement that is convenient or pleasing. It may
help to visualize two compact cars end-to-end to develop a
picture of this 5-foot by 25-foot bed in your mind's eye. Rather
than cultivating a whole large rectangle and then walking on
half of it, compacting the soil and damaging plant roots, these
narrower beds, once cultivated, never need to be stepped on
again. The original preparation takes many hours. But it can be
done in small sections when you have the time, and it only has
to be deeply cultivated once. After the initial cultivation you
will just add compost to the top three or four inches of soil, and
tend the plants from paths on either side of each bed.

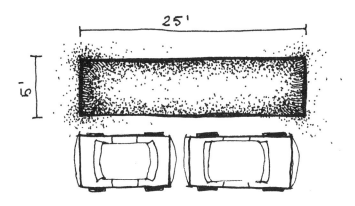

If you were to compare the cost, you would find an
organic/intensive garden more economical than a nonorganic
one. As the years go by it would become increasingly so, since
the need for fertilizers and pesticides to control the plants'
health increases in a nonorganic garden. The recurring ex-
penses of your organic garden would be limited to seeds, a pH
adjuster for the first three years (which I'll explain in step 4,
and some occasional phosphate, while your garden soil would
grow richer every year as you added free waste material.

Comparison of Initial Costs

Organic	*Nonorganic*
tools	tools
seeds	seeds
fence	fence
soil builders: rock phosphate, granite dust or greensand, bonemeal, manure	soil builders: peat moss, dried manure, granular all purpose fertilizers
2 × 4s and wire or boards for compost enclosure	rental or purchase of roto-tiller or tractor

Comparison of Recurring Costs

Organic	*Nonorganic*
seeds	seeds
lime or sulphur to correct pH (for two or three years)	fertilizers
rock phosphate (once every two or three years)	pesticides
	lime or sulphur to correct pH every year

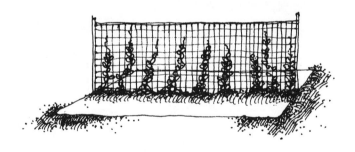

3

When to Start

FALL IS IDEAL

No matter what time of year the spirit moves you to begin a garden, there are always things you can do to get started. There is a preconceived notion among those who live where cold, snowy winters are followed by glorious reawakening springs that spring is the time to begin a garden. Actually, fall is the ideal time.

Summer activities are winding down and there are plenty of sunny but cool days left that are just right for strenuous digging. Waste materials like fallen leaves, dried stalks, and weeds are plentiful for layering into your garden beds and for starting a compost pile. There is time to plan the best layout for your garden, using whatever space you have most efficiently, and time to gather the necessary information about your particular growing season. A whole winter lies ahead of you to plan just what you will grow where, and to order seeds from catalogues that are a feast for winter-weary eyes.

During the fall, the university laboratories and experiment stations where you can have your soil tested are less busy and will give you quicker results. If you find your soil drastically lacking in any of the fertilizer elements (nitrogen, phosphorus, and potassium) you have time to gather organic materials to apply to your garden. Lime is best applied in the fall to raise the pII to between 6 and 7, the level at which vegetables grow best.

SUMMER IS OKAY

Next to fall, the summer is probably the best time to get started. You can actually explore other people's gardens to see how they are laid out and what various vegetable plants look like. Almost every gardener has some tidbit of information to offer, and you can learn a lot about which plants do well next to others by asking and observing.

Make a mental note of the vegetables you and your family really like to eat, so you won't waste space on those you merely think you ought to eat. Sample some that are not familiar and you may find one or two that you like and want to include in your own garden. Puchasing these vegetables from roadside stands in the summer also gives you a chance to observe which crops grow best in your climate.

Walk over the space that will be available for a garden, whether at home or in a community plot, and gather the necessary data on sunlight, water availability, and growing season. You can plan the shape of your garden, and if it is now field or lawn you can place thick six-to-ten-sheet layers of newspapers over the future garden beds to start the decomposition process. Weigh the newspapers down with stones and cover them with hay, straw, leaves, woodchips, or whatever waste material you can find that is aesthetically more appealing to look at on the ground than the newsprint.

Look around for sources of waste materials and start gathering them, so you can build a complete compost pile that will be ready for the garden you will be planting next spring. Neighbors' pet rabbits, dairy or chicken farms, and horse stables are good sources of nitrogen-rich manures. Seaweed is usually high in potassium and most of the trace minerals as well. Wood ashes from your fireplace or bonfire are an excellent source of potash, too. (Not ashes from your charcoal grill which will attract vermin, or from your coal stove, which are too high in sulphur.) The best sources of phosphorus are bonemeal and rock phosphate, and you will have to purchase these to get your garden off to a good start. Leaf mold is rich in all the minerals, so be prepared to stockpile autumn leaves for your compost.

SPRING WILL DO

If you must start in the spring then so be it, but be ready to accept disappointing results. It takes several months for a bed that has been double-dug and organically fertilized to be ready to carry plants through a full season. If you are going to spend the time and energy digging, you want to see some good results for your efforts. For this reason only I suggest that you start with a small bed, maybe 5 by 16 feet, about the size of a compact station wagon, and apply a commercial fertilizer at the recommended rate. Just this once, mind you! A soil test kit, available at most hardware stores, will give a reading of your soil pH to help determine the correct fertilizer formula.

Start seeds or seedlings of five to eight vegetables in your 80-square-foot bed. Lettuce, beet, and bean seeds, for instance, plus tomato, eggplant, broccoli, and/or pepper seedlings may all be purchased at a garden store. If they have onion sets (tiny onion bulbs), plant a row of these around the garden perimeter to confuse insect pests. At least a starter garden such as this will show you how nice it can be to pick and eat your meals fresh from a garden.

In anticipation of further digging in the fall, start gathering compostable materials and build compost enclosures using 2 × 4 posts with chicken wire, snow fencing, or boards around the sides. An enclosure that is three feet high with sides of four feet is just right for a backyard garden. You will want two of these eventually, side by side (see Step 6).

EVEN IN WINTER

If the pictures in a seed catalogue capture your fancy and inspire you to begin a garden, then by all means start planning, even if it's January and 10° outside. In order to establish whether or not you have the required six-hour minimum of sunlight, make note of the sun's arc. During the winter months it will form an angle with the horizon that is roughly half its angle with the horizon during the summer, and thus there will be fewer hours of sunshine. (See illustration.) Allow for bare trees that will be in leaf in summer which may create shade for part of the day. When you find the right sunny spot you can plan your layout and mark it off with stones. If there is a thaw that softens the earth sufficiently, you might even sink the corner posts for your compost enclosures and get that job out of the way.

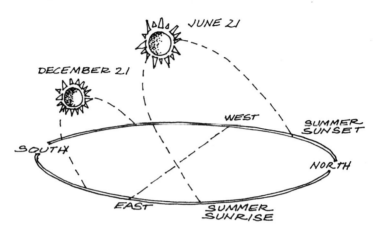

EARTH AND SUN, SHARING WINTER ARC AND SUMMER ARC OF SUN AT 40° LATITUDE

Order your seeds and, using the planting time and spacing under Step 11 in the next chapter, make a drawing of your garden on a large piece of graph paper. A week-by-week schedule of when to plant what can be a tremendous help when spring comes. If you can find a quiet afternoon to figure it all out and write it down, you will enjoy your garden that much more. You will still be confronted with the rush digging job in the spring, but you will be more prepared than if you had waited until spring to do anything.

4

Creating Your Garden Step by Step

Step 1

GATHERING INFORMATION

Sun

Before you start planning your garden you must know how many hours of direct sunlight you can count on in the space where you plan to grow vegetables. If you don't have a minimum of six hours of sun, you will get a very poor return for the time and effort invested. Sun, water, and properly prepared soil are equally important. If you shortchange your garden on any of these ingredients you are setting yourself up for disappointment.

Before you give up, however, check with your Town Hall to see if there is a community garden. In my own town probably half of the houses are shaded by stately trees which allow only an hour or two of sun in any one spot. A sunny community garden located on town open-space land now provides one hundred plots, 15 by 15 feet. Or, perhaps a neighbor would be willing to let you create a garden on a piece of his or her sunny land in return for picking privileges. A neighborhood garden could be both a catalyst for making new friends and a close-to-home outlet for a variety of creative talents.

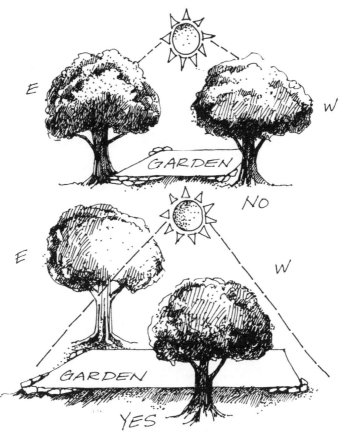

Growing Season

It is important to know the average frost dates in your climate and the approximate temperature range. Here in Southern Connecticut frost dates are officially given as May 3 and October 8, which gives us a growing season of 158 days. The length of the season can vary, however, and you may have a lot more growing time one season than the next. Last winter we were picking beet greens and spinach through the end of November because we didn't get a hard freeze until mid-December. A call to your county Cooperative Extension Service (see page 35) or your state Agricultural Experiment Station (which may be connected to your state university) will give the frost dates and the approximate temperature range for your climate.

16

Water

I'm sure I don't need to emphasize the importance of water. Growing vegetables without it is impossible. There are ways to make a little of it go a long way, which I describe in a later chapter on Garden Maintenance; but it is impractical to plan a garden far from a supply of water. An outlet close to your garden will make watering so easy that you won't be tempted to procrastinate or forget.

You will need a watering can and a garden hose with a fan spray nozzle. (The fan spray nozzle attached to your hose simulates a gentle rainfall, rather than allowing the water to pelt the ground in a hard, compacting stream.) If you are purchasing a watering can a Haws sprinkling can (see Step 3) which has an upturned head is best for watering seed flats or new seedlings. I prefer these two implements to a sprinkler, which is a notorious water waster and often does not reach the plants needing it most. The whole subject of watering correctly is dealt with in detail in the chapter on Garden Maintenance.

HAWS SPRINKLING CAN

FAN SPRAY NOZZLE

Step 2

DECIDE ON YOUR GARDEN SITE

Site Requirements

The perfect location for your garden is a level or gently sloping space which faces south, located well away from the roots or shade of trees, and convenient to your house and water supply. Do not choose a location near surface-feeding trees such as maples and willows. It must, of course, be in direct sun for at

17

least six hours each day. A steeper slope of more than 25° should probably be terraced to prevent erosion. As you dig your beds, use the stones that turn up to form small retaining walls. If you have logs or boards, use them along with the stones. In any case run your beds horizontally across the slope, not up- and downhill.

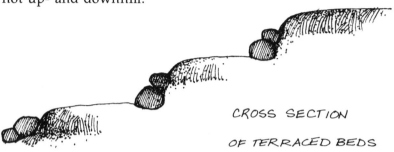

CROSS SECTION

OF TERRACED BEDS

Size

The size of your garden will depend on how many people you intend to feed and how many are willing to help you dig. I have a "base family" of three who are home all the time, and six others who come and go. My garden covers an area of 25 by 35 feet with roughly 600 square feet of planted beds, and we buy very few vegetables. I must admit that we don't grow all the winter squash, potatoes, dry beans, and corn that we eat; but gradually we are opening up more space. An old crabapple tree that we had to cut down last spring, for instance, has provided an additional sunny corner in our yard for growing more of these favorites.

The main thing to remember is START SMALL. Some friends of mine started with one bed 4-feet wide and 25-feet long, carefully prepared and lovingly tended, which yielded them all the lettuce, carrots, parsley, tomatoes, and string beans that their family of five could eat that summer, plus smaller amounts of onions, beets, and cabbage. They were delighted with this small garden because it was productive without being overwhelming.

Shape

As I have said, a garden doesn't have to be a rectangle. The amount of land available to you will tell you how big your garden can be; but the contour of the land and your sense of design will determine how many square feet actually become vegetable beds and in what shape. No matter what shape you choose, make your beds *between 4 feet and 5 feet wide,* a comfortable reach to the center of the bed from either side. I allow for generous 2-foot to 3-foot paths between beds so that tending them can be comfortable. Also, plants have a way of spilling over onto paths, which often end up half their original width.

You can make your garden L-shaped, T-shaped, E-shaped, a circle, a checkerboard, or you can make it a simple row of parallel beds, to name just a few of the possibilities. You can add more garden space by building trellises or a 6-foot fence for vine crops to climb. Six-inch reinforcement wire is good for melons, cucumbers, and tomatoes. (We found some rusting away at the town dump and put it to good use.)

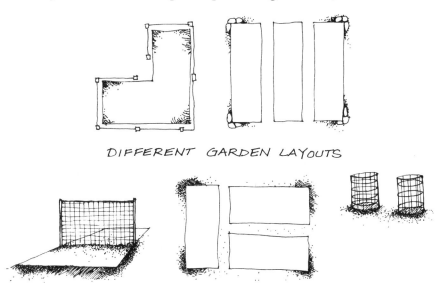

DIFFERENT GARDEN LAYOUTS

Step 3

PURCHASE TOOLS AND EQUIPMENT

There are hundreds of tools to choose from in stores and catalogues, and to the untrained eye it is difficult to know which are essential, which are optional, and which are really unnecessary. I have very few tools, but they are the very best and I reward the good work they do for me by taking good care of them. There is no need to buy many tools, but the few you buy should be good ones that will last.

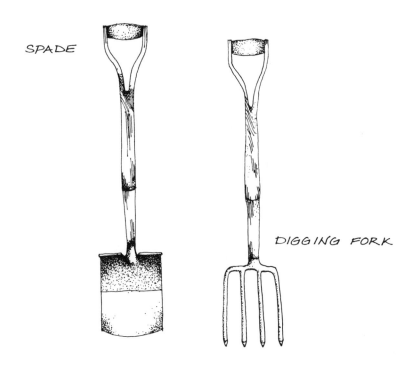

SPADE

DIGGING FORK

I recommend that you purchase a medium-size digging fork and spade at the very beginning of your gardening career. There are excellent English-made tools that are now available in the United States, and with proper care they will be with you for the rest of your life. The working end of one of these tools has a long solid neck into which the hardwood handle is tightly fitted. It is made from one piece of tempered steel and is absolutely unbreakable. You can sharpen the edge of the spade with a 59-cent file before using it, which makes any digging job much easier; and for the initial skimming of the ground in double-digging (see Step 9) a sharp edge is a must. These English tools may be purchased in the United States from:

Smith & Hawken Tool Company
68 Homer
Palo Alto, Calif. 94301

I have been unable to locate any other American distributor, but Smith & Hawken will ship anywhere in the United States and will send, on request, a beautifully drawn catalogue which describes the process by which the tools are made. Ordering these tools is well worth the trouble because they will outlast three or four sets of cheap ones.

In caring for all my tools I keep a bucket of sand moistened with old crankcase oil near the tool shed door. I dip the tools into this oily sand after each use, after first wiping them free of dirt with a burlap rag. This keeps them shiny and free of rust.

Here is a list of tools and equipment you should have.

Large Tools	Small Tools	Other
medium digging fork	trowel	marking stakes
medium spade	cultivator	twine
brush rake (fan-shaped)	hand clippers	waterproof pencil
wheelbarrow or cart		notebook
large burlap cloth		small basket
metal rake (straight edged)		garden hose with fan spray nozzle
		Haws watering can with "rose" nozzle

The burlap cloth is for carrying leaves to your compost pile and the small basket is for carrying the small tools, seeds, and miscellaneous items. Although I often prefer to use the tines of my digging fork to loosen the soil surface and smooth it for planting, a metal rake is easier on a tired back. The fan spray nozzle has many holes in it to simulate rainfall, rather than one adjustable opening for the water to pass through. It may be used with or without a watering gun (see illustration). The Haws sprinkling can is another English-made tool which can be mail-ordered from

Walter F. Nicke
Box 667G
Hudson, N.Y. 12534

Its rose nozzle, like the fan spray, has many holes and creates a gentle shower for seeds and delicate plants.

WATERING GUN

Step 4

HAVE SOIL TESTED

Soils can be acid or alkaline, or they can be neutral. On a range from 1 to 14, the lower numbers are acid and the higher are alkaline. The degree of acidity or alkalinity in your soil is referred to as the pH, which stands for potential Hydrogen. For the gardener's purposes it is only necessary to know that your pH should fall between 6 and 7.

PH LINE   ACID 1 ◄——— 6-7 ———► 14 ALKALINE
VEGETABLES
LIKE IT BEST
HERE

You can test the soil to determine its pH yourself or you can send it to a laboratory, but however you choose to do it you won't know what adjustments to make unless you know your soil's pH. Home test kits are available at hardware stores or through seed catalogues and are simple to use. From four different spots in your garden take a tablespoon of soil from 3 or 4 inches below the surface. Mix them together and let the soil dry out completely before you test it, usually at least four or five days. You will fill a test tube one-quarter full with soil, add an equal amount of a special liquid, shake to mix it well, let it settle a few minutes, and then compare the color of the liquid with a color chart provided in the kit.

Your county Cooperative Extension Service can tell you where you may have your soil tested in a laboratory, but usually the state university or Agricultural Experiment Station will test your soil without charge if you mail them a sample. You may have to wait several weeks for the results if you mail it in the spring because that's when everyone else is "thinking gardens"; whereas a fall soil test should bring a quick response.

If your soil is acid you can raise the pH one unit—from 5 to 6, for instance—by applying dolomitic lime at the following rates:

very sandy soil (will not hold together after squeezing in your hand)	30 pounds per 1,000 square feet
sandy loam (crumbly texture)	50 pounds per 1,000 square feet
loam (crumbly texture, holds together somewhat after being squeezed)	70 pounds per 1,000 square feet
heavy clay (holds together in a lump after being squeezed)	80 pounds per 1,000 square feet

Dolomitic lime is the best of the agricultural ground limestones to use in a vegetable garden because it contains magnesium, one of the essential microelements, as well as calcium. Avoid using quicklime or hydrated lime, which can destroy soil humus.

I have never gardened in alkaline soil, but I understand that you can lower the pH one unit by adding sulphur at the following rate:

alkaline soil	2 pounds sulphur per 100 square feet

You may also use naturally acid materials in your soil-building program, like peat muck from swamps, oak leaves, bark or sawdust, pine needles, or peat moss. In either case, acid or alkaline, organic matter tends to neutralize the pH, so each year of adding organic compost to your garden will result in a soil that is more nearly neutral.

When you are having your soil tested, ask for the levels of nitrogen, phosphorus, and potassium. The rates at which soil amendments containing these fertilizer elements should be applied are given in Step 5, but I would suggest adding them in the following order:

first: lime, preferably in the fall
second: manure—three to four weeks after lime
third: rock phosphate and granite dust or green-sand (for potash)—one month after manure
fourth: bonemeal and wood ashes sprinkled over the beds and forked into the top 2 inches at spring planting time

Adding lime in the fall where you dig your beds gives it the whole winter to work on your garden soil. It is also best to avoid applying it at the same time you apply other fertilizers; thus the time lapses between applications indicated above. If you are using dry, powdered manure, add it in the spring along with the bonemeal and wood ashes.

Step 5

FIND SOURCES OF ORGANIC FERTILIZERS AND WASTE MATERIALS

To start your organic garden you will need to locate some organic sources of the three fertilizer elements, nitrogen (N), phosphorus (P), and potassium or potash (K). Although some plants need more of one element than another, all three must be present in the correct ratio to achieve a soil medium which is conducive to good plant growth. If this sounds complicated, it is; but you needn't worry about soil imbalance after the first two or three years if you fertilize with a well-balanced compost (see Step 4), and make sure you have plenty of organic matter in your soil.

Nitrogen

Animal manures provide nitrogen and add organic matter to the soil, helping to build humus. Rabbit, poultry, horse, cow, and other livestock manures are all good for the garden. Dog and cat manures should not be used because they can contain harmful bacteria. Dry, powdered manure, though a good source of nitrogen, feeds only the plant, not the soil. (Remember, the first tenet of organic gardening is just the reverse.) Manure with bedding, such as you might find in a horse stable, is excellent because it also contains horse urine, which is even higher in nitrogen and potash than the solid matter. A forkful per square foot is a rough rule of thumb for using stable manure.

I apply a top dressing of horse-stable manure as my crops are finished in the fall or during the winter. It gets forked under in the spring. I also put whatever fresh manure I can find on my compost pile. Friends now save me their pet-rabbit and -goat droppings. It is also worth mentioning that in arid countries urine is about the only water available to moisten a compost pile and it serves as an activator, too. It speeds up the decomposition process and adds valuable potassium to the pile as well.

There are other sources of nitrogen which are available at an organic supply store; but the latter are few and far between. Since the U.S. Department of Agriculture is becoming more interested in organic farming and the needs of the small farmer, you may soon be able to learn of organic fertilizer outlets from your county Cooperative Extension Service agent. If you are lucky enough to find an organic supply store, you may have a choice of cottonseed meal, bloodmeal, chicken feather meal, fish meal, fish emulsion, liquid or granular seaweed, tankage, or hoof and horn. They are all organic sources of nitrogen. Unprocessed chicken feathers, hair, and coffee grounds will all supply nitrogen to your compost pile, as will fish scraps, but the latter may also attract vermin.

Phosphorus

Bonemeal and rock phosphate are the two most available sources of phosphorus. Bonemeal also contains nitrogen, while rock phosphate contains many trace elements. You will probably have to purchase either one at a garden or organic supply store in order to give your garden an initial dose of phosphorus. You should apply rock phosphate (not super phosphate which will disappear from your soil in a short time)

25

at the rate of 10 pounds per 100 square feet about a month after you have applied manure. Add a handful of bonemeal to each planting hole when planting tomatoes and other fruiting vegetables to assure healthy plants during your garden's early years. The decomposing organic matter in your soil and your compost will also make phosphorus available to the vegetables for years to come.

Potassium

Save the wood ashes from your fireplace, wood stove, or any outdoor wood-burning in a waterproof container. The potash will leach out very quickly if the ashes are left out in the rain. They are a rich source of organic potash and they also contain a significant amount of calcium, phosphorus, and magnesium, plus several other trace minerals. Think of an oak tree sending its tap root deep into the subsoil, drawing up the trace minerals into its wood, bark, and leaves. All the minerals can be recycled into the top soil by composting the leaves and the wood ashes in your compost pile. Top dressing with wood ashes is all right too, but the minerals will leach through the soil much more quickly than they would if they were chemically bound to organic matter in your compost.

Greensand and granite dust, available through organic supply stores, are also approved by most organic gardeners for adding potash to your garden. Apply these fertilizers at the following rates:

Greensand: 25 pounds per 100 square feet
Granite dust: 10 pounds per 100 square feet

Local Waste Materials

Take stock of other waste materials around you in addition to those already discussed. You will need materials for building compost and for mulching. Woodchips, sawdust, corn stalks, sea straw, cannery wastes (fish, vegetable, fruit), cobs, hulls, shells, and even hair cuttings from the barber shop will all be useful to the organic gardener. Get in the habit of keeping your eyes open for anything that looks like organic material going to waste and haul it home to your compost pile. I keep plastic bags in the back of my car for collecting any new discoveries.

Of course, the more common and abundant wastes like newspapers and autumn leaves are easy to accumulate and to use. Newspapers are good for keeping the weeds down in the paths between your beds, and a few of them shredded into your compost pile are perfectly acceptable. Autumn leaves are a gold mine for organic gardeners. They provide the bulk of the carbonaceous material in my compost pile, and will decompose in a pile by themselves into a rich leaf mold to mix with loam for potting soil.

If you can find a local farmer who sells his spoiled hay (wet when baled and, therefore, spoiled as feed) it makes a very clean and appealing mulch. Some of the hay seeds will germinate in your garden, but they will be easy to pull since the soil beneath a hay mulch is soft and loose. Salt hay, cut from the salt marshes, is weed free since marsh plants will not grow in upland soils and vice versa. It can be purchased from garden supply stores and is more expensive than spoiled hay.

For me the real challenge is to find things that are free and unused, and then be able to transform them into something useful.

Step 6

START BUILDING YOUR COMPOST
Steps 1, 2, 3, and 5 can really be done at any time of year. Since my preferred time to begin a garden is in the fall, however, I will proceed as if that is the time you have chosen to begin: You have sent off your soil sample to be tested and now, while you are waiting for the results, is the perfect time to begin building your compost piles.

What Is It and How Does It Work?
The lifeblood of organic intensive gardening is compost, and it will be your main fertilizer for many years to come. Making compost is really a speeded-up version of nature's soil-building process. Made from carbonaceous and nitrogenous materials that are allowed to decompose into humus, compost will provide all the elements essential for healthy plant growth. Your job is to gather these organic materials and layer them in a pile. The workhorses of the soil—worms and microbes—then

take over and set about the seemingly monumental task of converting the organic matter into humus. They do this at a steady tempo that releases small amounts of nutrients in a form that the plants can use. They continue to do this for as long as they have plenty of organic matter to work on.

When compost is used on your garden in its partially decomposed state, the microbes and worms keep working away, providing a balanced diet of nutrients to your vegetable plants. Instead of having to apply nitrogen, phosphorus, potash, and lime as you do when you begin a garden, and maybe a trace mineral fertilizer at different times and from different sources, you can add compost to your garden at any time.

In all fairness, there is a serious challenge facing you: that is to make enough compost to do the job. Even a small garden will require a lot of compost, especially if you intend to plant successive crops for eight or nine months of the year. This is why it is important to start your compost pile as soon as possible.

NEW ZEALAND COMPOST BOX

(BOARDS ON ONE SIDE ARE REMOVABLE)

How to Build Your Pile

Select a location near your garden, in a partially shaded area if possible. A compost pile should be kept moist and, therefore, must be located in the shade, or else it must be covered with some sort of tarp, black plastic, or a piece of an old rug to keep it damp. There should be enough space to hold two piles, three to four feet high and four feet on each side, one that you are currently building and the other finished and "cooking." It is not absolutely necessary to enclose a compost pile, but it will keep out inquisitive animals and the pile will heat up better than an uncontained one. In dry regions, compost is made in pits in the ground so that precious moisture is not lost. My compost enclosures are constructed with 2 × 4 uprights surrounded by snow fencing because I happened to have it; 2 × 4 posts surrounded by chicken wire or 1-inch wire mesh will work just as well. The accompanying drawing shows a neat compost box constructed of wood.

Here are some of the waste materials that can be composted:

Carbonaceous	Nitrogenous	Other
dry leaves	green leaves	seaweeds
dry weeds	green weeds	wood ashes
bark	coffee grounds	shredded newspapers
sawdust	tea leaves	cannery residues
woodchips	manures	
cobs	urine	
stalks	fruit peels and cores	
pits	vegetable residues	
eggshells	hair	
nut shells		
hulls		

Layering

First you must loosen the ground where your piles will be with a digging fork or pickaxe. This will prevent the build-up of an acid layer on the surface of the ground, which would inhibit the entry of soil microorganisms. Build the pile in layers, alternating carbonaceous with nitrogenous materials. Generally speaking, all dry leaves and stalks are carbonaceous and all green moist materials are nitrogenous. Animal wastes are nitrogenous. Although it is not vital to include manure in a compost pile for balance of soil elements, small amounts of it will speed decomposition. This is particularly true if you have many more dry leaves than fresh green waste or a layer of sawdust, which needs a lot of nitrogen in order to decompose. In nature the manures of animals in the wilds are widely scattered. Thus a scattering of manure, or a thin layer of it, is sufficient in a compost pile.

The first layer on top of your loosened earth should be branches or stalks (sunflower or corn stalks are perfect) which are slow to decompose and will thus assure air circulation at the bottom of the pile. Next a layer of green vegetation and kitchen wastes should be added. (No meats or fats, which attract vermin.) Cover this with a thin layer of soil; then dry leaves and any smaller dry materials, a layer of manure if you have it, more green vegetation, etc. Repeat until the pile reaches the top of the enclosure. Occasional layers of wood ashes "sweeten" the pile and add potash. One- to two-inch layers of soil assure the presence of microorganisms and prevent nitrogen from escaping into the air. The pile should be watered as needed because moisture is essential to microbial activity.

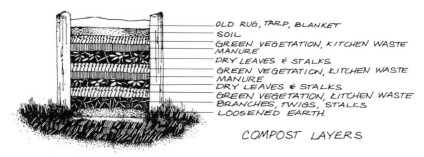

OLD RUG, TARP, BLANKET
SOIL
GREEN VEGETATION, KITCHEN WASTE
MANURE
DRY LEAVES & STALKS
GREEN VEGETATION, KITCHEN WASTE
MANURE
DRY LEAVES & STALKS
GREEN VEGETATION, KITCHEN WASTE
BRANCHES, TWIGS, STALKS
LOOSENED EARTH.

COMPOST LAYERS

The layering described here is intended as a guide rather than a hidebound process from which you cannot deviate. You can insert additional two- to four-inch layers of seaweed, for instance, or sawdust, or any other desirable organic material when you have it. Just remember to *alternate the carbon and nitrogen*—because carbonaceous materials decompose slowly and use up nitrogen in the process—and the other materials can go in at any point. In the fall when dry leaves are abundant, I put some of them in my compost pile, and the rest in a leaf pile to be added as needed throughout the year to balance the nitrogen loads of kitchen waste, weeds, and plant residues. A 12-inch layer of newly fallen leaves will quickly mat down to 4-inches, whereas leaves which have been piled for a few months will already be matted down and a 4-inch layer would be appropriate. A 4-inch layer of sawdust, on the other hand, will stay 4 inches for a long time and will need a layer of manure to decompose.

When your pile is complete it must be thoroughly wetted down so that it is moist, but not soggy, and then sealed with a

2-inch layer of soil and covered with an old rug or blanket if it is not shaded. Turning the pile after two or three weeks will speed decomposition by adding air to the pile, but it is optional. Turning also assures a more even decomposition, as materials on the cooler outside of the pile are shifted to the hotter middle. Eventually you may want to add a third compost enclosure to facilitate turning the "cooking" pile.

Next to double-digging your garden beds, gathering materials and building compost will probably be your most time-consuming garden chore. It would be impossible to make too much compost, however, for it is the key to growing healthy, nutritious vegetables in an organic-intensive garden. Each year you will spread about three or four inches of compost over your entire garden and work it into the topsoil. Heavy feeders will flourish if planted in a hill of pure compost. Each time you plant a successive crop after a heavy feeder you will want to replenish the compost again. In fact, the more you have the more you will use—for ailing shrubbery, sickly lawns, ornamental trees, and potted houseplants. And you'll wonder what you ever did without it!

Step 7

STOCKPILE MATERIALS FOR DOUBLE-DIGGING
Gather piles of the following materials for bed preparation in a place that is convenient to the garden.

dry stalky materials:	dried wildflower or weed stalks, sunflower or corn stalks, dry leaves
green waste materials:	grass or turf that you skim from the surface of your beds before digging, weeds, vegetable or flower residue
manure:	fresh or old cow, horse, goat, sheep, chicken, rabbit, or even shorebird droppings, if you happen to live next to the shore

Step 8

STAKE OUT YOUR GARDEN OUTLINE

Mark off the outline of your garden with stakes and twine, or with stones. Remember to make your beds no wider than 5 feet so you can reach the center of the bed comfortably from either side. Once you have gone to the trouble of aerating your beds by double-digging them, you won't want to step in and compact the loosened earth again.

Step 9

DOUBLE-DIG GARDEN BEDS

Now you are ready to begin building the backbone of your garden—a well-prepared bed. Most garden sites, whether lawn or meadow, have been compacted by feet and by millions of years of gravitational pressure. Your objective is to loosen the compacted soil to a depth of 16 to 20 inches. In the process you will add air as well as a "green manure" layer which will result in a "raised bed"; but the natural soil stratification will remain, with the topsoil on top and the subsoil beneath it. Double-digging or deep bed cultivation makes it possible to place plants closer to one another because their roots can now go down looking for nourishment rather than having to spread out horizontally.

Double-dig your garden beds as follows:

Select a 10-foot length of 4-foot wide bed to dig. Skim the top 3 or 4 inches of grass or turf from the surface of the bed. A good sharp edge on your spade will make this job possible, whereas you would quickly get discouraged with a dull-edged one.

Next, dig a trench across one 4-foot end of your bed, about 12 to 15 inches wide and a spade's depth. Put the topsoil from the trench in a wheelbarrow and dump it just beyond the other end of the 10-foot section you are digging.

Plunge your digging fork to its full depth, if possible, into the bottom of the trench and rock it back and forth to loosen the subsoil. Do this several times so that the soil is loosened the whole width of the trench. Remove rocks as necessary (some soil is full of them).

Put a layer of organic materials on top of the loosened subsoil: a bunch of stalks or dry leaves, followed by a sprinkling of manure, followed by a layer of turf or grass skimmings, and any other green wastes. Chop these materials with short up-and-down thrusts of your spade.

Dig a second trench alongside your first, and throw the topsoil from this second trench on top of the organic materials in the first trench.

Proceed to loosen the subsoil in the second trench, put in a layer of organic materials, and cover with topsoil from a third trench.

Repeat this procedure to the end of the 10-foot section you are digging, filling the last trench with the topsoil removed from the first trench.

You now have a 4 by 10-foot bed with a curved or raised surface because you have put a layer of organic matter 8 inches beneath the soil's surface and you have added air to the soil. This raised bed gives you more planting surface. The organic matter will decompose slowly, releasing nutrients for the plants' roots as they reach down into the loosened soil.

33

DOUBLE DIGGING

SKIM SOD FROM BED SURFACE

EDGE BED ALL AROUND

1   DOUBLE DUG SECTION

2   OPEN TRENCH

3   SOIL FROM FIRST TRENCH TO GO INTO THE LAST

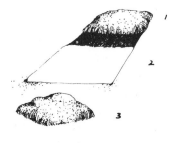

RAISED BED AFTER DOUBLE DIGGING.

Double-dig as much of your garden as you have the time and energy to do in any one session. It doesn't have to be done all at once but as I have already pointed out, in the fall you have the ideal weather to do the job and no rush to get it done in time to plant. You won't be planting until the following spring.

34

PLAN WHAT TO GROW WHERE IN YOUR GARDEN

Climate Zones

The United States can be divided into nine hardiness zones. The planting times and schedule given here are for the middle zone, where the average minimum temperature is −10° to 0°F. (−12° to −18°C), and the last spring frost date is May 3. In colder zones you would have to plant two to three weeks later, in warmer zones two to four weeks earlier.

There are many factors that can influence climate, such as altitude, degree of exposure to prevailing winds, proximity to the ocean, annual rainfall, type of soil, and sunlight. These factors can create variations in climate of as much as two zones within the same geographical area. There are even mini-climates within your own yard that allow daffodils to bloom on one side of the house while the ground is still frozen on the other.

Cooperative Extension Service County Agent

It would be wise to call your Cooperative Extension Service County agent and ask him about the climatic variations in your county. With the exception of Connecticut, every state lists its county agents in the county-government section of the telephone book. In Connecticut you can obtain the county agent's number by calling your district Congressional representative's office, listed in the U.S. Government section of the telephone book.

The Cooperative Extension Service is the local arm of the U.S. Department of Agriculture and serves farmers and gardeners alike. In addition to providing accurate information about your growing season, your agent may be able to help you locate sources of organic fertilizers. Just be sure to identify yourself as a backyard vegetable gardener who is interested in building soil organically.

Planting Times

When you have decided which vegetables to include in your garden, the following lists will help you decide when and how deeply to plant, and how far apart. You should set your dates

PLANTING ZONES

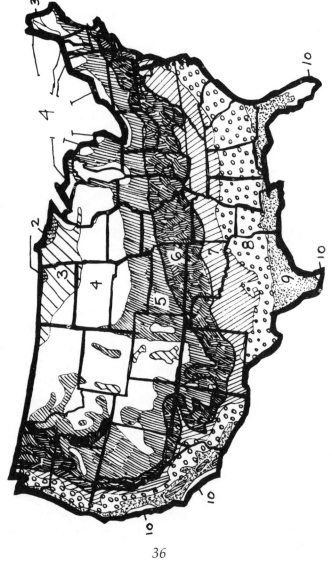

MINIMUM TEMPERATURES	
ZONE 2 -50/-40	
ZONE 3 -40/-30	
ZONE 4 -30/-20	
ZONE 5 -20/-10	
ZONE 6 -10/0	
ZONE 7 0/10	
ZONE 8 10/20	
ZONE 9 20/30	
ZONE 10 30/40	

two to four weeks earlier, or up to three weeks later, depending on the information obtained from your county agent. These are dates for planting vegetables to be harvested in the fall, and several successive planting dates for some vegetables to assure a continuous supply. By planting short rows at two or three week intervals you won't be inundated with too much of anything at one time.

April 1	*April 15*	*May 1*
lettuce	turnips	lettuce
radish	potatoes	radish
peas	onion sets	peas
spinach	beets	spinach
fava beans	broccoli (plants)	
roquette	cabbage (plants)	
	carrots	
	celery (plants)	
	peas	
	spinach	

May 15	*May 20*	*June 1*
snap beans	tomatoes (plants)	squash (plants)
squash	peppers (plants)	cucumbers (plants)
cucumbers	eggplant (plants)	melons
leeks (for fall)		(seed or plant)
parsnips (for fall)		Brussels sprouts
		(for fall)
		carrots
		snap beans

June 15	*July 15*	*August 10*
snap beans	carrots (for fall)	lettuce (for fall)
broccoli (for fall)	snap beans	spinach (for fall)
cauliflower (for fall)	snow peas (for fall)	turnips (for fall)
rutabaga (for fall)	beets	radish (for fall)
		roquette (for fall)

In this list "plants" indicate that seedlings can be purchased or that seeds should be started indoors or in a cold frame at an earlier date, usually indicated on the seed packet.

Planting Seeds Directly in the Garden
In the following table the spacing of plants is closer than you will find recommended on seed packets or in the gardening

37

books. This is because you will be planting in beds that have been deeply cultivated, so the roots will be reaching down for nutrients instead of spreading out horizontally. From the "days to mature crop" column you can tell if it is possible to grow more than one crop in the same space during one growing season. The wide variation in days to maturity is due to there being early and late varieties of plants. Choose yours on the basis of when you want to be able to harvest it. An early maturing broccoli would be your best choice for spring planting, for instance, because it does not do particularly well in hot weather. You can choose a variety that takes longer to mature for your fall harvest.

Vegetable	Depth	Space Between Plants After Thinning	Days to Mature Crop
beans, lima	1"	4"–6"	70–80
beans, snap	1"	2"–3"	45–60
beans, fava	1"	6"	60–75
beets	1/2"	3"	45–60
broccoli	1/4"	12"–15"	50–90
cabbage	1/4"	12"–15"	55–120
carrots	1/4"–1/2"	1"–3"	55–110
celery	1/4"	6"–8"	5–6 months
collards	1/2"	18"	120
cucumber	1/4"–1"	12"	50–65
eggplant	1/4" to 1/2"	18"	75–90
lettuce	1/4"	8"	45–80
mustard	1/2"	4"–6"	35–45
onion (seed)	1/4"–1/2"	3"–4"	110–130
peppers	1/2"	12"	100–120
potatoes	3"	12"	40–75
pumpkins	1"	1'–1 1/2'	90–100
radish	1/2"	2"	28–36
rutabaga	1/4"–1/2"	6"–8"	80–100
spinach	1/2"	3"	40–50
squash, summer	1"	6" (1 1/2' between hills)	50–65
squash, winter	1"	6" (1 1/2' between hills)	85–105
tomato	1/4"	18"–24" (staked)	54–90
turnip	1/4" to 1/2"	2"	35–50

Succession Planting

Early summer plantings of vegetables for fall harvest can fill the spaces occupied by the early spring-planted lettuce, spinach, fava beans, and peas. Late-summer plantings of lettuce, spinach, and turnips for fall can fill the spaces left by your early carrots, broccoli, onions, and potatoes. Through succession cropping you can assure yourself of both maximum production from a small space and a constant supply of fresh vegetables well into the cold weather. Crop succession is dealt with more thoroughly in chapter 10.

Drawing

After you've decided what to plant, but before planting, make a drawing of your garden to scale on graph paper, and mark in pencil what you intend to plant and when. Then write out a calendar for yourself so that all you will have to do come spring is refer to your planting calendar. Keep both the drawing and the calendar in your notebook and mark any changes you make at planting time. Keep them for the following year. You will probably make changes, but it will be much easier having something to work from.

Planting Schedule

The following calendar helped me plant my garden last spring. I kept it posted in my kitchen so I could refer to it daily and do what was scheduled on a particular day. The dates given are for southwestern Connecticut but could be adjusted for other zones by adding or subtracting the appropriate number of weeks.

March 1:   In cold frame, start lettuce, 2-foot row

March 15:   Indoors start tomatoes, peppers, eggplant, celery in flats. In cold frame start another 2-foot row of lettuce; in garden start spreading compost and turning where possible.

March 26:   In garden plant first row of peas (10-foot). In cold frame start broccoli and kohlrabi.

39

April 1: In garden start spinach (Bed 1), radish (Bed 5), roquette and fava beans (Bed 3).

April 10: Transplant lettuce from cold frame to Bed 3. In garden plant second row of spinach, second row of peas, and lettuce.

April 15: In cold frame start herbs (basil, calendula, thyme, etc.), and annuals (marigolds, zinnias). In garden, start more radish, beets (Bed 1), and carrots (Bed 3).

April 30: From cold frame transplant broccoli and kohlrabi to Bed 4. Put seedlings started indoors into cold frame to harden; start cantaloupe seeds in cold frame. In garden plant third row of spinach and peas, second rows of carrots (Bed 3) and beets (Bed 1), and onion sets and radish. Thin lettuce.

May 10: Plant first row of beans (15-foot).

May 15: Transplant tomatoes, eggplant, peppers, basil, and calendulas from cold frame into garden. In garden start cucumbers and squashes, nasturtiums and leeks. Plant cukes on a trellis at the end of pepper row to provide midday shade.

June 1: Plant pole limas along east fence, second row of beans, bush limas (Bed 2), shallots among kohlrabi. Transplant melons from cold frame to northeast corner. Start broccoli, Brussels sprouts and cauliflower in a supply garden or cold frame for fall harvest.

June 15: Plant more beans, transplant celery (Bed 3), and replant peas if first planting is finished. Start rutabaga.

40

July 1:   Mulch peppers with grass clippings and apply bonemeal.

July 15:   Plant carrots (Bed 5) for fall and mulch lightly with hay to be sure they don't dry out. Plant more green beans. Replant snow peas along north fence for fall; transplant broccoli and Brussels sprouts to where fava beans and early carrots were. Water peppers with fish emulsion weekly.

August 10:   Plant lettuce in cold frame for fall, spinach along edges of Beds 1 and 4, beets where first row of beans have finished, and turnips where second row of beans are as soon as they are finished.

August 30:   Plant roquette and transplant lettuce. Plant radish in cold frame.

Doing all of this planning may take several winter afternoons or evenings, but it will be time well spent. When spring comes you won't have that frantic feeling of having forgotten everything you had so carefully thought out in the dead of winter. And planting will take half the time because you know just where to go and what to do.

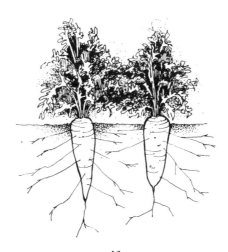

GARDEN PLAN

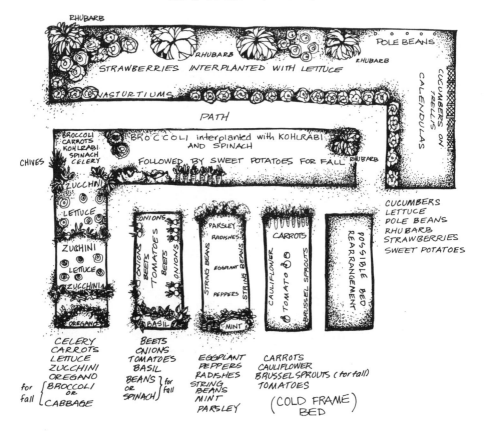

RHUBARB

POLE BEANS

STRAWBERRIES INTERPLANTED WITH LETTUCE

RHUBARB RHUBARB

NASTURTIUMS

CUCUMBERS ON TRELLIS CALENDULAS

PATH

BROCCOLI CARROTS KOHLRABI SPINACH CELERY

BROCCOLI interplanted with KOHLRABI AND SPINACH

FOLLOWED BY SWEET POTATOES FOR FALL

RHUBARB

CHIVES

ZUCCHINI

LETTUCE

ZUCCHINI

LETTUCE

ZUCCHINI

OREGANO

ONIONS TOMATOES BEETS ONIONS

BEETS ONIONS

BASIL

PARSLEY RADISHES

STRING BEANS

EGGPLANT

PEPPERS

STRING BEANS

MINT

CARROTS

CAULIFLOWER

TOMATO

BRUSSEL SPROUTS

POSSIBLE BED REARRANGEMENT

CUCUMBERS
LETTUCE
POLE BEANS
RHUBARB
STRAWBERRIES
SWEET POTATOES

CELERY
CARROTS
LETTUCE
ZUCCHINI
OREGANO
for { BROCCOLI
fall { OR
CABBAGE

BEETS
ONIONS
TOMATOES
BASIL
BEANS } for
OR } fall
SPINACH }

EGGPLANT
PEPPERS
RADISHES
STRING
BEANS
MINT
PARSLEY

CARROTS
CAULIFLOWER
BRUSSEL SPROUTS (for fall)
TOMATOES

(COLD FRAME)
BED

Step 11

PLANT YOUR GARDEN

Planting your garden will not take place until spring; but since we have just discussed spacing and planting depths it seems a logical time to talk about how to plant. Some vegetable seeds may be sown directly in the garden, while others will be transplanted into the garden as seedlings. Let's divide the former into small, medium, and large seeds and deal with them separately.

42

Planting Seeds

Large seeds like peas, beans, and squashes may be planted where they will remain throughout their productive lives. Peas may be planted in double rows close to the fence they will climb on. Bush beans do better in single rows. They grow quite tall and full, and may have to be supported—a string running along either side of the row, attached to two-foot high stakes at each end, works well.

Pole beans and squashes should be planted in groups of six to eight seeds clustered in a circle (a "hill") 8 inches in diameter. I have found that beans do not like overcrowding, so when they are 4 to 6 inches high I thin out the weakest plants, leaving four to grow around one pole. I also thin the squash, leaving the four strongest seedlings. I plant a new hill of squash each month so that if borers get the early plants I will have more coming.

To sow medium-sized seeds like beets, spinach, radishes, and turnips, make parallel furrows, 4 inches apart and 1 inch deep, and place the seeds an inch apart in these furrows. I use my metal rake to make the furrows and cover the seeds lightly with soil, tamping each row with the flat side of the rake's tines to firm the soil covering. When the seedlings reach 4 to 6 inches I thin them to stand 3 inches apart, and use the thinnings for salads.

Small seeds like carrots may be sown in the same way, except that the seeds are too tiny to handle individually. Open one corner of the seed packet and tap the packet gently until the seeds start to flow out. Then move down the rows, tapping a small amount of seed into each furrow. You will have to thin the carrot seedlings to stand 1 inch apart when they are 4 inches tall, which takes a little time but is well worth the effort. Onions may be planted this way too, but thinning or transplanting onion seedlings is painstaking work. When cutworms once mowed down my entire crop the very night after my labors I decided to plant onion sets next. These small bulbs cost more than seeds, but they can be pressed into the soil at 4-inch intervals just where you want them to grow, and they will sprout within days. Furthermore, the cutworms don't seem to care for them.

The net effect of planting in these close rows is what appears to be a solid wide band of vegetable greenery. It makes the best use of your garden space and is actually quite orderly when you want to pull a few carrots or beets at a time. You do not leave large empty spaces for weeds to encroach because neighboring plants seem to fill the spaces immediately with their foliage.

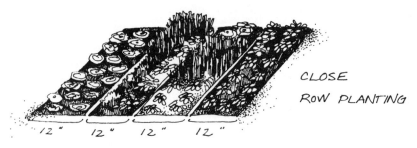

CLOSE
ROW PLANTING

12"   12"   12"   12"

Sow lettuce and cabbage-family seeds in short, single rows, 2 or 3 feet long, or in small planting boxes. Lettuce loves to be transplanted and you will have enough lettuce seedlings from a 3-foot row to fill a 6 by 4 foot bed of lettuce planted in a solid grid, the seedlings planted 8 inches apart in all directions. Cabbage seedlings should each be transplanted into a depression that resembles a horse's hoofprint, spaced 1 foot apart. In fact, the bed will look exactly as it might if a horse had walked over it. Water will collect in these depressions, assuring the seedlings plenty of moisture; and when the plants are 8 to 10 inches high, fill in the depressions with soil. The mature cabbage head will therefore rest on the bed's surface, instead of at the end of a long stem that would ultimately be unable to support the cabbage's weight.

Starting Seeds Indoors
In the five coldest zones of the country certain vegetables are started indoors because they take a long time to become established plants, or because the seeds will not germinate until the soil temperature is 70°. Tomatoes, peppers, eggplant, and celery fall into this category. Started indoors six to eight weeks before planting in the garden, they will have several sets of leaves before they are set out. You can get a head start on warm

weather vine crops like cantaloupe by starting them indoors two to three weeks before outdoor planting time in individual peat pots or peat pellets, those compacted discs that swell when soaked in water.

To start seed indoors do not use soil straight from your garden; it will cake and harden unless it is mixed with a lighter material. Use a mixture of equal parts of garden loam, strained compost, or peat moss and builder's (coarse) sand. I use wood flats lined with newspaper, or 4½ by 6½-inch plastic planting trays. Cover the seeds with a fine sifting of your seed bed mixture. I have had good results with a fine covering of sphagnum moss sifted through an old cake sifter, which seems to prevent damping off, a condition fatal to newly emerged seeds. After watering I cover the seed flats with newspaper until germination begins. Then I place them under a Gro-lite or in a sunny south window.

The soil should be kept moist and the flats turned or tipped to face the sun daily to assure even growth of the seedlings, since they will always grow toward the sunlight. Transplant the seedlings to stand eight to a planting tray when they have their second set of true leaves. Be selective and choose only the biggest, healthiest plants, discarding the scrawny ones. Otherwise you will end up with too many plants for your garden.

These seedlings should be hardened off before being planted in the garden. Take them outside for a few hours each day in warm weather, lengthening the outdoor time each day until, after a week or so, they are accustomed to the outdoors. I harden my seedlings off in the cold frame. (Cold frames are discussed in the later chapter on Extending the Growing Season.)

Transplanting

Remember when transplanting, do not hold the seedling by its stem. Hold it by a leaf, or cup the root ball in your hand. The stem is the "neck" or lifeline, and squeezing will very likely damage it and result in a sickly plant with poor disease resistance. Dig a hole that is larger than the root ball and set the plant in the hole. Now hold it by a leaf to keep it standing up straight, and gently fill in all around the plant, pressing the soil gently but firmly in place with your fingers. Water it thoroughly.

Transplanting should be done on a cloudy day or in the late afternoon to preserve the seedlings' supply of moisture. Also, water seeds and seedlings daily during their first few weeks or until plants are established. The top inch or two of soil can dry out very quickly in bright sunshine, and lack of moisture means death to newly germinated seeds.

A LIVING MULCH

Step 12

MULCH IN YOUR GARDEN

Mulch is material used to cover the soil, keeping in moisture, discouraging weed growth, and preventing loss of nutrients into the air. Mulches are an optional item in an organic/ intensive garden, because in an intensively planted garden the plants themselves form a "living mulch." The leaves of each mature plant touch those of neighboring plants, forming a canopy that shades the earth beneath. No other mulches are absolutely necessary, but there are certain conditions under which I find a mulch very helpful.

When to Mulch

Seeds planted in early summer for fall crops that will germinate in the hot weather should be lightly mulched with hay to prevent the soil from drying out. Beets, tomatoes, and other potash-loving plants benefit from a mulch of seaweed or comfrey leaves (more about comfrey in the chapter on Weeds) after the plants are established. A light mulch of hay beneath squash, cucumbers, and tomatoes will prevent the fruit from rotting as it ripens on the ground. The roots of vine crops growing on a trellis or fence may also be kept cool with a hay mulch.

Some gardeners swear by a mulch of dry oak leaves, which are rather prickly and take a long time to decompose, to discourage slugs. Mulching the paths of your garden with 6-sheet-thick layers of newspapers covered with hay or straw will mean less weeding, a neater appearance, and a nice surface to walk on in your bare feet.

Building Your Soil With Mulch
Mulches provide more organic matter for the tireless microorganisms in the soil. Worms will actually draw nutrients from surface mulches down into the soil where they are available to the roots of vegetable plants. While a garden bed should first be dug and prepared before using a mulch, if you have plenty of mulching material there is no reason not to use it after the bed is aerated and fertilized with compost. Where soils are either very sandy or heavy clay, a mulch will improve the tilth of the soil. It will moderate changes in soil temperature and make easier the job of keeping your garden's appearance aesthetically pleasing. In the late fall I often cover my garden beds with seaweed or horse manure and stable bedding. This "winter mulch" adds organic matter when it is forked into the top of the beds in the spring.

Step 13

HARVEST YOUR PRODUCE
Harvesting vegetables is, generally speaking, a matter of picking them at the right time and eating them in a variety of ways. There are several important things to remember, however.

Visit Your Garden Daily

Don't let your garden get ahead of you. By inspecting it daily you won't be surprised by discovering a 2-foot zucchini or beans as big as carrots. The old admonition about watched pots never boiling certainly doesn't apply to vegetables. Once a plant starts to yield edible fruit you can almost see them grow. A 2-inch baby bean can reach 6-inch perfection in forty-eight hours. Zucchini squash can quadruple in size overnight. Crisp, delicious lettuce or spinach can bolt (go into their seed production phase) and become bitter in a few days of hot weather.

If you don't want to be caught off guard and have to spend the evening freezing quantities of overgrown, less than perfect vegetables, keep on top of your garden production. It is easier to freeze or can small batches of just-ripe vegetables, or give away a few vegetables in their prime to grateful friends, than to try finding recipients for a bushel of over-the-hill produce. In that case your compost pile will be your best bet. That's one of the best features of growing your own food organically— nothing ever goes to waste, because it can always be recycled through composting.

When to Pick

Another thing to remember is that there is a right time of day to pick most vegetables. It is best, for instance, not to pick lettuce and other delicate greens in the heat of midday, for they will wilt beyond recall if you can't get them into the refrigerator immediately. Beans, on the other hand, should never be picked until after the morning dew has evaporated from their leaves. Bean plants when handled while still damp develop mildew or rust, and become more susceptible to insect infestations. I pick my bean plants clean at least once a week, and they keep producing all summer long.

Never pick a melon until it falls off in your hand when you pick it up. The sugar content will be at its peak then. I have tried ripening cantaloupes on my kitchen windowsill and they are never as good; in fact, they're quite tasteless. By the same token, leaving peas and beans too long on the vine or corn on the stalk gives the carbohydrates time to convert to starch.

When people remark that fresh-picked corn or peas in their prime are "sweet as sugar," they are stating the truth. An old lima bean is a starchy, tasteless bean that belongs in your compost pile or in next year's supply of seed.

Vegetables harvested in their prime not only taste better, they also freeze better, dry better, and make better pickles and preserves. Vegetables that are slightly overripe can be canned, but, with the exception of tomatoes, I prefer to freeze green vegetables. I also store winter vegetables like carrots or rutabaga and winter squash in the garden (see next section), or on my chilly but enclosed back porch. For me the taste of a canned vegetable is just not worth spending hot summer days and nights over a hotter stove, when I have another choice. I am grateful to be living in the era of freezers!

Cold Weather Harvesting

Let's hope you have included in your garden a selection of vegetables for fall harvest. Certain ones like kale and Brussels sprouts actually taste better after a few frosts, so don't pick them too soon. They can even be harvested after an early snowfall. Beets, carrots, and turnips can stay in the ground long after frost has killed their tops. Before the winter settles in for good, dig the carrots and lay them together in a trench, covering them with loose dirt and a bale of hay or a pile of leaves to protect them from freezing. In this way you can harvest carrots all winter.

Tomatoes picked green at the first frost warning may be stored in single layers in a flat box lined with newspaper, and covered with more newspaper. The ethylene gas which they exude and which causes them to ripen is trapped between the newspaper layers, and the tomatoes turn red slowly. A home-grown tomato, even when ripened under newspaper, is a much tastier vegetable than one of the pale, hard, mechanically harvested varieties that has traveled hundreds of miles to reach you.

Step 14

REPLANT WITH SUCCESSIVE CROPS

There is nothing that frustrates me more than seeing empty spaces in a vegetable garden during the growing season. In

Step 11, I touched on succession-planting in planning your garden, and in this last step I will expand on this concept, so important to maximum production. Too many people, for instance, feel that their garden is finished once Labor Day has come and gone. But there are many vegetables that will continue to furnish delicious fresh food well into the cold months of November and December, with a minimum of effort on your part.

Supply Garden

Keep a small section of your garden, 2 feet by 4 feet, for a supply garden or nursery. Here you can start small quantities of lettuce seed and all the seed for your late cabbage-family crops so they are at hand for transplanting into those empty spaces. You should have a supply of lettuce seedlings ready for "catch-cropping" (filling an empty space) throughout the season. When your fava beans are taking their time about ripening due to a very cool May and June, it won't matter that the Brussels sprouts have to wait a week or two longer, because they are growing happily nearby and will only be moved a few feet when the time comes to transplant them. They'll hardly know they've been moved.

Overlapping

As you harvest spinach and lettuce, give a thought to pulling plants out every 12 to 15 inches, the correct distance apart for broccoli seedlings. You can plant the seedlings in the empty spaces while the spinach and lettuce are still growing in the same row. Because spinach and lettuce are light feeders, you won't even have to add more compost to the bed. Late in the summer you can plant lettuce seedlings from your nursery or supply garden beneath the broccoli, where they will be partially shaded from the late summer sun. At that time you should add compost to the soil, because broccoli is a heavy feeder and will have depleted the soil of many nutrients. Light and heavy feeders are discussed in more detail in the chapter on Crop Rotation in Part II. Other combinations for overlapping are covered in Companion Planting.

50

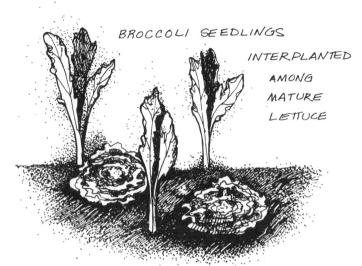

BROCCOLI SEEDLINGS INTERPLANTED AMONG MATURE LETTUCE

This concludes the fourteen steps to getting started. It's not necessary to read the second half of this book until after your garden and compost pile are under way—unless you are hanging on every word and can't put it down! I have tried to walk the fine line between giving enough information and direction without overwhelming you with unnecessary detail.

One of the very nicest things about gardening organically is that the soil improves every year, so the taste and quality of your vegetables will, too. As time passes you will want to find out more about growing things and how to improve the way you are growing them. Part II offers information that will help to make your garden better. So when your beds are completed and the vegetables are growing happily, relax under a tree somewhere and read on.

II

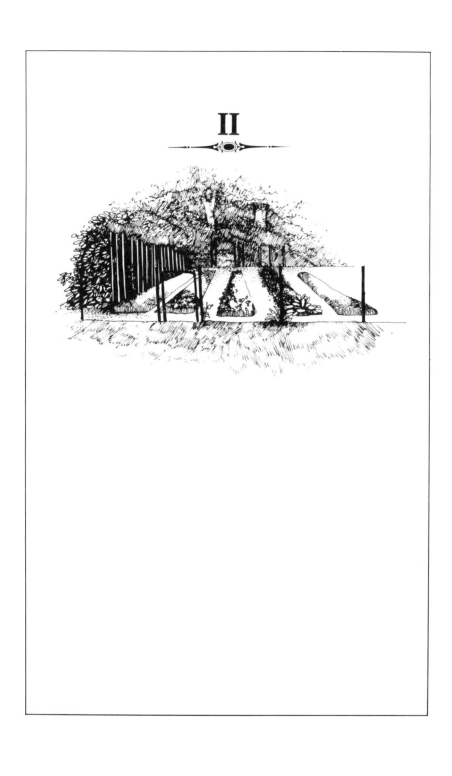

5

Understanding Soil Structure

Soil Horizons

If you were to dig a foot-deep hole with straight, smooth sides, you would see that the soil has layers of different colors. Soils can be shades of red, gray, or brown, but generally speaking the top layer would be the darkest tone and the bottom would be the lightest. Soils that contain a great deal of sand are more uniform in color. The top layer varies in thickness, depending on where you are digging. If it is eight inches deep you are in luck. If it is only three inches deep you will have to work longer at making the soil suitable for growing food. It takes hundreds of years to build a few inches of topsoil (literally, "top soil") through the natural process of the vegetations' growth and decay. Composting emulates this process, but obviously takes a much shorter time.

Topsoil consists of organic matter that has decomposed with the help of bacteria, fungi, and molds—the microorganisms referred to in earlier chapters—and earthworms which eat bits of decomposing matter and excrete castings particularly rich in nitrogen. Topsoil contains the soil elements needed to support plant growth and is looser in structure than the lighter colored "sub soil" beneath.

Subsoil is mostly clay and tightly compacted, making it

impenetrable to all but the toughest, most determined root systems. It contains important minerals, however, which are needed by most plants. They are drawn up into the topsoil, to some extent, by the movement of earthworms along passageways left by root systems that have decayed. Deep-rooted trees draw minerals up into their leaves, which then fall to the surface of the ground where they decay, and the minerals are released into the topsoil. Deep-rooted weeds do the same.

In double-digging the soil layers are loosened, but left in their original positions, with the topsoil on top and the subsoil beneath. Seeds and seedlings have an easier time of finding the nutrients in the rich topsoil and, as the plants mature and develop a greater need for minerals, their root systems find the minerals more easily in the loosened subsoil.

Rocks may be present throughout the soil layers in various sizes. Phosphate in the soil comes from rock which has been weathered through the millennia. The action of water and acids in the soil breaks rocks down very slowly. Thus it is best to remove most of the rocks from a garden bed since they are obstacles to root growth and release their phosphorus too slowly to be a significant aid to plant growth. Add crushed rock phosphate to garden soil every three years, instead.

Elements

There are seven macro- and nine microelements that are all necessary for healthy plant growth. In addition to the fertilizer elements nitrogen, phosphorus, and potassium, whose roles and sources were discussed in chapter 4, there are four other macroelements—oxygen, hydrogen, carbon, and calcium. The first three come from the air, or from water vapor in the air or the soil, and you should see to it that they are present by cultivating (aerating) well at least once a year, and watering. The calcium comes from lime or bonemeal which you must add to the soil also.

The micro or trace elements that are important in healthy plant growth are boron, chlorine, copper, iron, manganese, magnesium, molybdenum, sulphur, and zinc. Soils that contain plenty of organic matter usually supply plants with as much of each trace mineral as they seem to need. If you are continually building your soil by adding a well-balanced compost you should not have to add any microelements.

Healthy Soil

A healthy soil, then, contains all sixteen elements. It contains organic matter and the microorganisms which feed on this organic matter, digesting it into humus and in the process releasing the elements in a form that the plants can absorb. It contains moisture, which is retained by the organic matter until the plants need it, and air spaces into which plant roots can grow easily. Your job is to provide the organic matter, and aerate, water, and lime when necessary: nature does the rest.

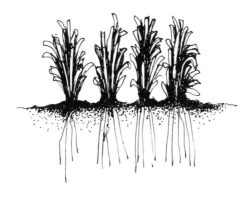

6

Organic Insect Control

What to Look For

In order to control insect predators in your garden, you must first know what you are looking for. There are three stages in the life of most insects—egg, larva, and adult. In the larval stage they are voraciously hungry, and that is when they do the most damage to plants. When you see moths or beautiful butterflies flitting among your vegetables, they are probably looking for the right place to lay their eggs—which is on the plant their larvae most prefer to eat. When you see a cluster of eggs on the underside of a leaf, or what appears to be a single brown egg attached to a stem, these have been carefully deposited by the moth and will soon hatch into tiny hungry larvae.

There are literally thousands of different insects, enough to study for a lifetime; but in a vegetable garden you will probably only be concerned with a few. Within a year or two you will know which ones they are, and at that point it would be wise to purchase a book on insects filled with color illustrations (see Bibliography) so you can identify the enemy.

Controls

If you get in the habit of making a daily inspection of your garden you will quickly notice the changes that take place. Leaves with holes or edges chewed away will alert you to the presence of hungry insect larvae. Although some larvae are perfectly camouflaged, like the cabbage worm that is the same velvety green as the cabbage leaves, others, like the yellow bean beetle larvae, can be seen on the underside of leaves. There is nothing safer than a quick pinch with gloved fingers for disposing of these creatures. An even better way to control chewing insects, however, is to keep a lookout for clusters of eggs usually found on the undersides of leaves which are being eaten, and apply the same quick pinch technique.

In the case of some of the larger larvae, or caterpillars like the tomato hornworm or the parsleyworm, you probably won't see them until they have grown large and beautiful. It is difficult to kill such a magnificent creature, but steel yourself, remove it, and step on it. Or, if you have children, they will be fascinated to keep the parsleyworm in a jar, well-fed with celery or parsley leaves, while they watch the larva form into a chrysalis and then metamorphose into a black and yellow swallowtail butterfly.

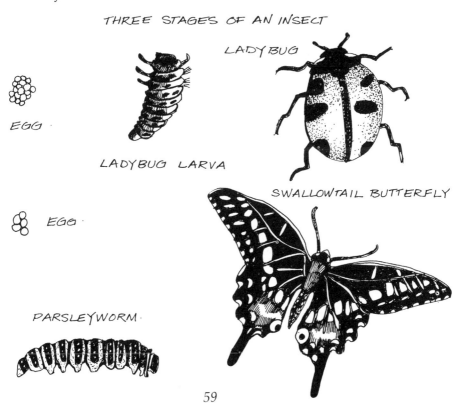

THREE STAGES OF AN INSECT

LADYBUG

EGG

LADYBUG LARVA

EGG

SWALLOWTAIL BUTTERFLY

PARSLEYWORM

There are certain insects that only come out after dark. Slugs and cutworms, for instance, are night eaters who vanish by morning, leaving only a trail of slime and leafless stems, or a wilted young seedling cut off at the base and lying beyond recall on the earth. A night raid with a jar in hand (slugs are too slippery to pinch) is the best approach to getting rid of slugs that are already in residence. Slugs do not like the prickly feeling of an oak leaf mulch. Crush oak leaves in your hands or underfoot and sprinkle them around the plants which are under attack. Or, place some lime under a board or newspaper or in any dark place near where slugs are doing damage. In the daytime the slugs will seek the darkness and will smother in the lime.

Cutworms can be routed out of the dirt close by the be-headed plant, where they are curled up digesting their dinner, and squashed under foot before they do any more damage. A toad in your garden will eat thousands of these nocturnal pests. Give him the shade of an overturned flower pot propped up on one side to sleep in somewhere in your garden during the daytime, and he'll stay the summer. Lizards and even a box turtle will eat pests in the daytime, too.

Birds will do a wonderful job on insect worms and grubs in your garden, particularly during the spring and early summer when both baby birds and insect larvae are most plentiful.

A variety of herbs and flowers mixed in among your vegetables create a profusion of aromas that confuse any insect. Each moth or butterfly is looking for the right plant on which to lay its eggs, and a cabbage moth, for instance, will not lay an egg on a broccoli plant if it smells like mint or onions. I regularly plant basil, thyme, dill, oregano, tarragon, mint, and chive plants here and there throughout my garden. I also plant nasturtiums and marigolds to deter nematodes (little root worms) and allow nicotiana, coreopsis, borage, and rudbeckia to seed themselves year after year. Any smart moth or butterfly usually gives up on my garden and goes where he can find his target more easily. Only a few lucky ones find what they are looking for.

If you have certain plant diseases year after year, like bacterial wilt on your cucumbers or mosaic on your tomatoes, you can select resistant varieties from the seed catalogues. It will narrow your choice of varieties, but it may actually be easier to have fewer to choose from!

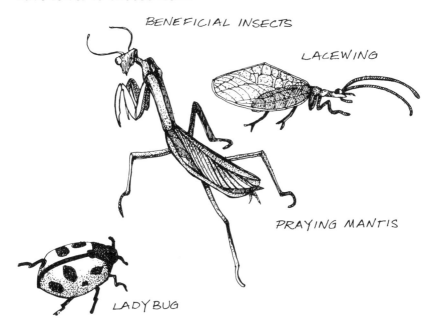

BENEFICIAL INSECTS

LACEWING

PRAYING MANTIS

LADYBUG

There are certain friendly insect predators that will work quietly along with you to keep your "bad" insect population down. A praying mantis will eat thousands of insect eggs, scale pests, aphids, beetles, and grubs. One tiny ladybug, I am told, will eat forty to fifty aphids a day. The pale green lacewing fly will also eat enormous quantities of aphids. Certain seed catalogues have advertisements of ladybugs for sale, and most garden supply stores will be able to tell you the closest source of supply. Praying mantis egg cases can be found in fields in winter and brought to your garden to hatch in early summer. The cases are golf-ball size and a light brown that is usually the color of the weed stalk to which they are attached. Bear in mind that these friendly insect predators will only stay around your garden as long as they have enough to eat. When the supply runs short they'll be off to greener pastures. In the Bibliography I have listed the names and addresses of biological control sources.

Spraying plants with water from the hose at high pressure will dislodge aphids and other sucking insects. Many of them will find their way back, so the process must be repeated daily until they are gone. Another very effective insect control is a 1 or 2 percent soap solution made with a mild dishwashing liquid like Ivory, and applied with a hand mister. The insects seem to choke on the soap solution.

There are a few other tricks in controlling insects which I have found to be successful and pass along to you to try. Toothpicks or any other small sticks placed alongside the stems of seedlings prevent the cutworms from cutting through the stem. This is less work and much less unsightly than cutworm collars made from paper cups or old tin cans.

If a batch of tiny beet or spinach seedlings is demolished one by one by some unseen predator, wait a few weeks and plant a second batch. By that time the predator (most likely a hatch of insect larvae) has usually moved on to another stage in its life cycle. Or, start your spring spinach in September, cover it with leaves and hay during the cold months, and around mid-April you'll have bright green tasty spinach leaves ready for picking.

To foil the squash borer make successive plantings in May, June, and July so that as each succumbs to the borer the next group of plants is beginning to produce. If you haven't space to do this, then slice the main squash stem open with a razor blade near the wilting leaves' stems, destroy any borers inside and cover the wound over with dirt. New roots will form and the plant will revive—if you found all the borers, that is.

Perhaps the very best insect control is a healthy soil, because it produces healthy plants. Insects can sense sickly plants which are not getting enough of the elements, and they prefer to eat these sick ones because they are higher in carbohydrates. Healthy plants will usually survive an insect onslaught with a little help from you.

7

Crop Rotation

There are good reasons why you should not plant the same vegetable in the same place year after year. Each one requires a slightly different balance of nutrients (elements) and will eventually deplete the soil of its particular favorites if the soil microbes aren't given time to replenish the supply. Also there are disease-causing organisms that will build up in the soil if one vegetable is grown there continually. It is wise to rotate your vegetable beds each year, particularly the members of the heavy-feeding cabbage family and potatoes.

Givers and Takers

There are "givers" and "takers" among the plant families. The givers are the nitrogen-fixing legumes, beans, and peas, which take nitrogen from the air by means of the bacteria that live in nodules on their roots, and fix it in the soil. In my small vegetable garden I rotate peas and several different kinds of beans throughout the garden. Before planting I shake the seeds in a jar with an innoculant powder (which I order along with my seeds through a seed catalogue) in order to assure good nitrogen fixation. When the plants have stopped producing I cut them off, leaving the roots with their nodules in the ground to decompose, and I throw the tops of the plants in the compost pile.

Here is a list of "givers" and "takers":

Givers	Takers	
	Light Feeders	*Heavy Feeders*
beans (all kinds)	Root vegetables: carrots, beets, radish, turnips, parsnips, rutabaga, salsify	Vine crops: squash, melons, cucumbers
peas		Leaf vegetables: chard, spinach
alfalfa		
clover	Leaf lettuce and other salad greens	Cabbage family: broccoli, Brussels sprouts, cauliflower, cabbages
rye	Peppers	
peanuts		Leeks
		Tomatoes, potatoes, eggplant
		Corn

Recycling Elements

There are limited quantities of each element in the world around us, and once you have captured some of them for your own use in your vegetable garden it makes sense to hang on to them: In making compost, elements are constantly recycled into the garden. Some of each element goes into the vegetables that we eat and thus is used by our bodies. The rest of the plant contains elements too, however, and by composting the part we don't eat we make these elements available to future plants.

Sheet Composting

In very sandy soils where water and fertilizer elements drain through the soil rapidly, "sheet composting" is the best method of retaining organic matter and valuable elements in the soil (see illustration). In sheet composting your garden paths are compost troughs (instead of piles) where you deposit leaves, plant residues, weeds, and kitchen wastes. Since aeration is not a problem with sandy soils, you walk on these paths throughout the summer, even as they are filling up with composting debris. In the late fall the topsoil from this year's beds is tossed onto the debris-filled paths, forming next year's beds. In this way you are constantly recycling organic matter into the top 12 inches of your garden. The organic matter holds both moisture and elements where the plants can use them, rather than letting them drain away.

Cover-Cropping

In order to give their soil a rest organic farmers—as opposed to backyard gardeners—plant a crop of nitrogen fixers like alfalfa, clover, or vetch every third year, and then till it into the soil to replenish both nitrogen and organic matter. By cover-cropping or planting this "green manure" crop for one whole growing season, these farmers recycle nitrogen and other elements found in the organic matter as it is turned back into the soil. Nothing is taken out of the soil for a whole year, while a good deal is put back in.

In a small organic vegetable garden you can grow continually if you replenish your beds with compost, a winter mulch, and an occasional double-digging, which, after two or three years of growing plants, takes maybe a tenth of the time it did originally. If you are unable to make enough compost, plant winter rye late in the fall—just scatter the seeds over your beds—after having tested your soil, adding any necessary fertilizer elements. In the late spring you can semi-double-dig; that is, when the rye is about 8 inches high pull it out and layer it in 8-inches under, as you would layer in materials during double-digging.

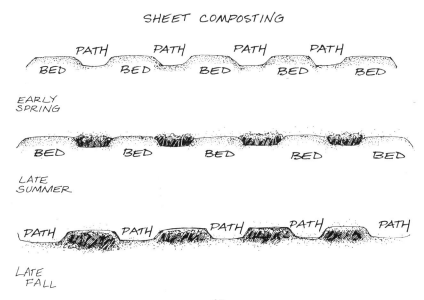

SHEET COMPOSTING

EARLY
SPRING

LATE
SUMMER

LATE
FALL

65

8

Companion Planting

Some plants will grow better in close proximity to certain other plants. Just as there can be "bad chemistry" between people, there are plants that do not like being next to certain other plants and they will show this by growing very poorly. Entire books have been written about companion planting (see Bibliography), but I will deal only with those that I have found to be significantly successful or unsuccessful combinations.

Vegetable Companions

I will never, for instance, plant a row of potatoes without a row of bush beans right next to it. The Mexican bean beetle and the Colorado potato beetle, the most common insect pests to attack these vegetables, do not get along and they seem to drive each other away. Horseradish planted at the corners of potato beds protects the potatoes from other insects. Remove the horseradish when you dig your potatoes, or it will become permanently established and very difficult to evict.

If you do not plan to have potatoes in your garden, then plant your bush beans with celery, beets, or cucumbers close by. All beans dislike onions and will grow poorly if they are too close to them. But a wide row of carrots should have a chive plant here and there, or a row of onions or leeks next door. Members of the onion family repel the carrot fly and its larva which attacks the carrot roots. Carrots also grow very well near tomatoes and lettuce, but don't accidently spill a packet of dill seed nearby, as I once did, because there is very bad chemistry between dill and carrots and neither will grow.

Beets, beans, and kohlrabi are excellent companions. Other members of the cabbage family—cauliflower, broccoli, Brussels sprouts, collards, and kale—will benefit from being close to celery, which seems to deter the white cabbage moth. This is the delicate creature that lays the eggs that hatch into those beautiful velvety green worms with the incredible appetites. A sprig of mint placed on newly planted cabbage-family seedlings will confuse the moth into going elsewhere for a day or two, but this is hardly practical as an all-summer deterrent.

I always plant early icicle radishes and nasturtiums near my cucumbers, melons, and squash. I allow several radishes to go to seed, which repels insects and provides me with next year's supply of radish seed, as well. The nasturtiums, incidentally, are really their most beautiful in the fall when their brilliant orange or pale yellow and pink flowers nod above a carpet of soft green leaves. For an indoor treat put them into the hottest water you can run from your tap right after picking and they will last in the house for several days. Nasturtium flowers are also a colorful and tasty addition to salads and their seed pods can be pickled as capers and used in sauces for meat and fish.

Flower Companions

In addition to nasturtiums among the vine crops, I plant several other flowers not only for beauty, but as pest deterrents as well. Marigolds are in every bed. It takes a year or two for the chemical secretions from their roots to condition the soil to the point where nematodes (tiny root worms) will not live in it. Once you have grown marigolds everywhere in your garden, however, you should not have a soil nematode problem. Marigolds are particularly useful to tomatoes and beans.

Nicotiana, or tobacco plant, has white flowers and a lovely fragrance, most noticeable in the early evening. It also has sticky stems and leaves that trap aphids, white flies, and other tiny flying insects. I use it as a trap crop, pulling it out when it has collected its fair share of insects. Nicotiana seeds itself so easily that I actually have to weed most of the seedlings out because I have too many. The plants grow from one to three feet tall.

67

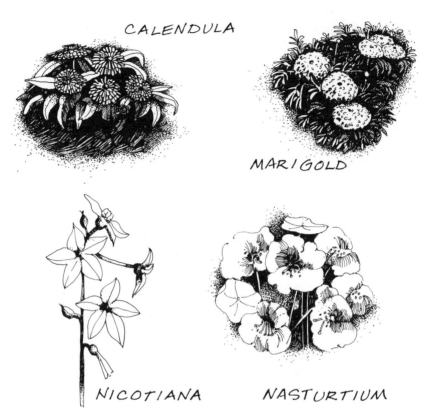

CALENDULA

MARIGOLD

NICOTIANA   NASTURTIUM

Pot marigolds or calendulas, which seldom grow taller than a foot, are placed around the periphery of my garden to keep the neighborhood dogs from leaving their calling cards. They are also the preferred food of cutworms and can be used as sacrifice plants next to tender vegetable seedlings. They come in a wonderful range of colors, from pale creamy yellow through deep orange, and make a wonderful bouquet on your kitchen windowsill.

Two volunteers that regularly come through my compost pile are coreopsis and the gorgeous rudbeckia, gloriosa daisy. I weed out all but a select few of these three-feet-tall flowers, but leave enough to attract the bees. The deep red flowers of beebalm at the garden gate, and scarlet runner beans climbing on tall poles, act as bee lures, too. Once in the garden the bees move on to pollinate the vegetable flowers. A garden should be a beautiful place, and the flowers guarantee it.

Herb Companions

One of the most satisfying vegetable herb combinations is tomatoes and basil. Both grow so happily together—the basil lush and fragment and the tomatoes incredibly delicious—that I wouldn't think of planting one without the other. (Rub basil leaves on your skin if you are troubled with mosquitoes.)

Mint is a nice addition to any garden if you can keep it under control. Besides its strong smell, which adds to the confusion of flying insects, its taste is refreshing as you chew it while tending the garden.

I also plant oregano in my garden near the broccoli, and parsley near the carrots. Both combinations seem to be beneficial.

9

Weeds

You will have come a long way on your gardening journey when you begin to look at weeds with a curious if not appreciative eye. Weeds are plants out of place; but they can tell us a lot and do good things for us if we will stop looking at them merely as a nuisance to be gotten rid of. A tidy, weed-free garden is not necessarily the most productive garden, anymore than a fastidiously clean house is the best home for creative minds. There are many reasons to be grateful to weeds.

Weeds as Soil Builders

Weeds grow best in poor soil. They are nature's way of re-building soil that has been overused or disturbed. When river banks are excavated for sand and gravel deposits, weed plants will appear within a year or two and begin the slow restoration of topsoil through their growth and decay cycle. Weeds have longer and tougher root structures that can reach down and out into the soil looking for nutrients. When they die back, their root systems decay, leaving a network of air spaces in the soil. Nitrogen-fixing vetches or other leguminous weed plants which will replenish the soil's nitrogen are among the first to appear. Left to its own devices, land that has been overgrazed by livestock will restore itself in several years in the same way.

Weeds as Indicators of Soil Condition

By becoming familiar with certain weeds, you can tell at a glance just what kind of soil they are growing on. They can indicate both the pH and drainage capacity of the soil. Golden rod, for instance, grows in alkaline soil, while cinquefoil and sheep sorrel thrive in an acid soil. Comfrey will grow in clay soil; field mustard, morning glory, and quackgrass in hardpan. The sedges and smartweed will grow in poorly drained soil. It is nature's intention to keep soil covered with plants or their detritus to prevent soil erosion. For this reason there are plants that will grow in almost any soil except sandy deserts. A balanced soil that is being fertilized with compost and used for growing vegetables will discourage weed growth because of the weeds' preference for soils that are long on some elements and short on others.

Weeds as Compost and Mulch

Weeds will be a staple in your compost pile. In fact, for awhile they may be the only material available for composting. When green they will contribute nitrogen; when brown and dried they will still add carbon. As the quality of your soil improves and you have fewer weeds in your garden, those that you do have may be pulled and left lying on the beds to dry in the sun and decompose right there. Young weeds have the right carbon-nitrogen ratio, and will decompose without robbing soil of nitrogen.

Low-growing weeds like purslane can also act as a mulch, shading your garden soil during extremely dry spells. Working in a garden in California during the third summer of a serious drought I was instructed to cut the tall weeds down to a height of three or four inches instead of pulling them. Pulling those weeds out would have disturbed the roots of their vegetable companions and loosened and exposed more soil, permitting precious moisture to evaporate. Leaving three inches provided a mulch which conserved soil moisture.

Weeds as Food

Most of the vegetables we eat today began somewhere as weeds and came under cultivation because they tasted good.

There are many wild weed plants growing today which are good to eat. Violet and dandelion leaves, both high in vitamin C, may be added to early spring salads. Lambsquarters are good either raw or cooked like spinach. The stems of young burdock taste very much like broccoli. Comfrey, considered a weed under certain conditions, may be eaten in a variety of ways: cooked as a green vegetable, blended with fruit juice for a nutritious pick-me-up drink, or made into tea. In a course I once took on urban ecology, our class of thirty collected almost an entire meal from wild weed plants growing on a vacant city lot.

COMFREY PLANT

Special Weeds

Comfrey is impossible to extract from a garden bed because of its 6- to 10-foot roots. This same incredible root system, however, is responsible for comfrey's many beneficial qualities, if you can find a place outside the garden where it can grow without getting in the way. (Mine grows not far from my compost pile in partial shade.) Comfrey roots bring up elements from deep in the subsoil, notably phosphates, calcium, iron, and potash. Comfrey leaves may be cut to within inches of the ground four times a season and still grow back again. I use the first cutting to line the trenches where I plant seed potatoes, the second I use as a mulch around my tomatoes; the third cutting goes under my raspberries or blueberry bushes; and if there is a fourth, I either add it to the compost pile or dig it into the soil where next year's onions will be planted. I feed the comfrey plants with horse or cow manure each fall to assure four cuttings the next summer, too.

Sonchus or sow thistle, considered a weed by nongardeners, was permitted to remain until it began to crowd neighboring vegetables in the California garden mentioned earlier. It was considered beneficial to the lettuces and other plants to have it growing nearby. Its thistle seeds attracted birds to the garden, and its roots added silica to the soil.

All of the information in this chapter is intended to give you a new perspective on weeds, and to relieve any paranoia you may have about the need to dispose of them. Weeds are really friends; but they must not be allowed to overwhelm. The diversity they add to the community of plants in your garden will, in the long run, be more of an asset than a liability.

10

Planning for Maximum Production

Choosing Seeds

Seed catalogues are available on request, free of charge, from dozens of seed companies. How to select seeds to make the most of your garden space from the dozens of choices in these catalogues, or even which catalogue to choose as your main source of supply, can stall your whole garden planning operation. I must admit that I still end up ordering more seeds than I need, no matter how carefully I plan, because they all sound so marvelous. (I keep extra seed from one year to the next in a glass jar in the freezer so they are not wasted.)

It stands to reason that a seed company in your geographical part of the country, that is your growing season zone, should have seeds appropriate for your garden. Comstock Ferre in Wethersfield, Connecticut, is my source for perennial plants like asparagus. I use Johnny's Selected Seeds in Albion, Maine, for most of my seeds, even though they are in a colder zone, because they specialize in short-season varieties. This means I can harvest more vegetables of different varieties, which is more important to me than winning first prize for size at a country fair. Johnny's is the only seed company I know of that espouses the principles of organic gardening, and makes a sincere effort to obtain seeds from organically grown plants. They also have nice recipes and a wealth of other useful information.

Assuming you have listed those vegetables and fruits you like to eat, and starred those which are "musts" for your garden, look through a seed catalogue from your zone to see what the possibilities are. You may want to send for more than one catalogue just so you have a basis for comparison. (See the list of seed companies and their addresses in Bibliography.)

Crop Succession

You will find that a head of iceberg lettuce takes 85 days to reach maturity, while leaf lettuces may be picked in 45 days. In our New England growing season of 158 frost-free days it would be impossible to grow more than one other vegetable in the same space where the iceberg lettuce grew. By comparison, a planting sequence of Black Seeded Simpson or Prizehead lettuce (45 days), followed by zucchini squash (50–80 days), allows a third crop—turnips (35 days)—to be grown in the same space. The zucchini are started while the lettuce is still growing, and the first lettuces picked are those heads closest to the zucchini seedlings, making space for them to grow. Here are other suggestions for three-crop sequences:

radishes – bush beans – kohlrabi
spinach – broccoli for fall – roquette
peas – cucumbers – radishes
lettuce – beets – late summer squash
spinach – cucumbers – lettuce
radishes – fava beans – Brussels sprouts
lettuce – eggplant – turnips

In choosing seeds for tomatoes and corn, bear in mind that you do not want them to come all at once. Select early, mid-season, and late varieties which will guarantee both an early supply, and one that never stops until the last green tomato has ripened indoors. Do not plant three rows of bush beans all at once, or you will have them coming out your ears for a month, and then have none. Bush string beans come earlier than pole beans, and lima beans will be later than both. Planting some of all three at approximately the same time will give you at least one kind of bean all summer long. An early and late planting each of carrots, beets, broccoli, and kohlrabi

75

will furnish you with enough of these vegetables all summer without being inundated. When you do have more than you need of any one vegetable, pick it at its prime and freeze what you can't eat that day.

Interplanting

In chapter 8 on Companion Planting, I mentioned several plant combinations that will grow happily in the same bed at the same time. To save space and achieve maximum production, for instance, carrots and onions may be grown in several adjacent rows, 4 inches apart, while flanked by lettuce or backed by a row of staked tomatoes. Lettuce, beans, and carrots all occupy different levels of the same bed: the carrot roots develop underground, lettuce hugs the first 6 inches above the ground, and beans hang on plants up to 18-inches tall. Radishes can be sown in the same space with any slow-germinating vegetable such as carrots or parsley, since they will be eaten long before their companion feels crowded. Tomatoes can share a bed with keeper carrots for an entire season. Beans, celery, and kale can spend a season sharing the same garden space. Remember that diversity is fundamental in intensive planting: it is what keeps plants healthy by not depleting the soil of any one element, and it keeps insects confused.

A feel for both spacing and timing will come after a year or two of vegetable gardening. Mistakes are often the best teachers. Overcrowding results in poor air circulation and often brings insect infestations. Empty spaces are an invitation to weeds. Don't be afraid to thin out, and "catch crop" whenever you see bare soil. (See chapter 4, step 14.)

Eat Seasonal Vegetables

Eating habits can become ruts which are difficult to get out of. It really doesn't make sense to eat nothing but frozen peas, beans, corn, and spinach in January, when we could be eating fresh beets, carrots, rutabagas, winter squashes, and kale stored right in or near the garden. (See next chapter.) Broadening your range of vegetable choices to include those that may be eaten fresh in winter will improve the nutritional caliber of your diet. It may take some time, especially if you have a family of finicky eaters, but plan on growing one or two new vegetables each year to see which ones your family will take to without too much fuss. Many of those winter-hardy vegetables can be eaten in soups, breads, and desserts instead of "as is." A whole new kind of menu might evolve one or two nights a week, featuring fresh winter vegetables in these new forms. There are wonderful vegetarian cookbooks filled with recipes and suggestions to help you. Combining your own frozen, dried, or canned vegetables and fruits with your seasonal winter ones can save you the cost of buying expensive out-of-season fresh produce at the market.

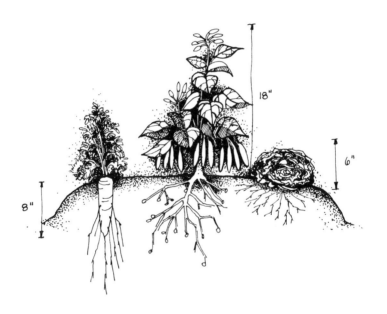

11

Extending the Growing Season

Cold Frames

Of all the experiences I have had in growing food, probably the most satisfying is raising lettuce throughout the winter in our cold frame. I admit to feeling quite smug as I serve our guests a green salad in December or early March, and can't resist announcing that "the salad is from the cold frame." It always evokes the desired incredulous response, and gives me the opening I need to explain that it's really possible to grow fresh greens almost all winter in this climate.

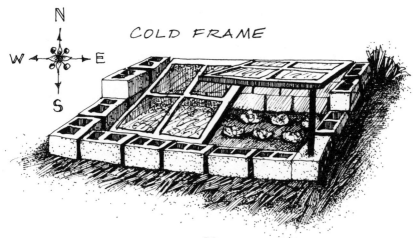

COLD FRAME

During the first winter of our cold frame, I remember thinking that all was lost when I went out to inspect my lettuce after several grey days of hard-frost temperatures, and the crop had turned a dark, dead green beneath a frosty coating. Two days of brilliant winter sun provided the heat and light it needed to return to its former bright green self, however. "A miracle," I thought; but it turned out to be a miracle that has repeated itself over and over. Lettuce actually goes into dormancy from December to February, but then it starts growing again as the sun's arc gets higher and the days grow longer. By the time I am ready to use the cold frame for new seeds in March, two-thirds of the lettuce has been eaten, and by late April when I need cold frame space to harden off tender seedlings, the lettuce is just about gone.

A cold frame is an outdoor minigreenhouse with a slanted transparent top which faces south. My children and I built ours of cinder blocks, 2 × 4 boards, and three second-hand storm windows. The whole thing cost us about $90, not counting our time.

There are many different designs for cold frames: plywood boxes that stand right in your garden with glass over the top slanted to an angle of 45°F. (7°C.) to catch the winter sun; holes in the ground lined with cinder blocks or boards, and covered with the same slanted glass; windows propped up at an angle against the south side of your house, with sides made of bales of hay or old boards. There are also vinyl "pods" and small thermostatically controlled, self-venting houses, some of which are commercially available. There are several books listed in the Bibliography which give detailed instructions on how to build a cold frame. Our experience, including our mistakes, may be helpful to you also.

We purchased the three old storm windows, 60 by 30 inches, for $3.00 each at a housewrecking company. We then dug a hole 18 inches deep, lined the sides with cinder blocks—four-blocks high at the rear and two-blocks high at the front—and built a wood frame inside the cinder blocks to accommodate the dimensions of the three windows placed side-by-side. The windows rest on slanted boards running from front to back (see diagram). Our one big mistake was placing the windows together on their long sides, because I have a tough time reaching the back of the cold frame without stepping in it. Five feet is just too far to reach, while 30 inches would have been comfortable. Using old windows meant using window glass, which is very breakable. I managed to get through a mid-winter broken glass crisis by taping double layers of clear plastic dry-cleaner bags over the broken pane. I have since removed the panes that were left unbroken after three years and replaced them with a clear vinyl that has an inner lining of chicken wire for strength which I stapled onto the old wood window frames. If necessary I will try acrylic panels next!

Starting Early

Starting seeds indoors, as outlined in chapter 4, Step 11, will extend the growing season and make it possible to grow plants that are not hardy in the cold. Melons require such a long hot season that I can't be sure they will ripen in time unless I start them early indoors in individual peat pots to minimize the shock of transplanting later. Sprouting sweet potatoes, and then putting the sprouts in several 6-inch flower pots to root into plants, makes it possible for me to grow sweet potatoes here in Connecticut, in spite of the Extension Service agent's recommendation against it. If I send for sweet potato plants through they mail they are half-dead on arrival and take several weeks to recover. Instead, I set two sweet potatoes, bottom halves submerged, in glasses of water in mid-March. To encourage sprouting, which takes quite a while to get started, I keep the glasses of water on a hot tray set on "low." Once they start, the sprouts will keep coming for weeks and will develop into large healthy plants by their early-June planting time. If I keep them going long enough indoors it is not always necessary to harden them off, although most years I do harden them off in the cold frame. I harvest them in early October, leaving three or four days after digging for their skins to harden before storing them on my cool back porch.

Vegetables in the Winter Garden

In the last chapter I mentioned the possibility of eating fresh garden vegetables in season year round. Cabbages and kohlrabi can stand a light frost. Brussels sprouts and kale actually taste better after several frosts. Kale can be kept going in a cold frame all winter. Carrots, beets, turnips, and rutabaga may be left in the ground, covered with 12 to 18 inches of hay and leaves, and dug as needed. Or, if you are short of protective mulch material, they may be dug and stored together in special trenches in one corner of the garden, first covered lightly with soil, then with hay and leaves. Jerusalem artichokes, leeks, parsnips, and salsify may also be dug throughout the winter if kept covered in the same way. While not exactly extending the growing season, storing vegetables through the winter right in your garden means access to fresh vegetables that you would otherwise have to buy.

12

Garden Maintenance

Like a child, a pet, a house, a car, or anything else that is important to you, a garden must be cared for regularly. If you plant your garden and then leave it to its own devices while you take a month's vacation, you will be in for disappointment. Weeds, which don't need regular watering the way young vegetables do, will establish themselves and thrive. Insects will probably have a field day. Unpicked vegetable plants will stop producing fruit and concentrate on setting seed instead. In the summer heat you may just decide to give up and forget the whole garden project, which would be too bad considering all you can gain from having a garden. Sharing your garden with a friend or neighbor could prevent this from happening. A garden is a very personal thing, however, and you must either include your friend in the planning from the beginning, or limit your summer vacation to a week or ten days at the most.

Plant Hygiene

Keep your garden clean by keeping the paths clear of weeds and piles of debris. Clear paths give a garden a semblance of order, and keeping them mulched with newspaper and lightly covered with hay not only looks appealing, but feels good to bare feet.

Thin out any weak-looking plants which invite insect infestations. Remove any diseased plants, like those infested with bean beetles, and plants with club root, mosaics, or wilts. I throw any suspect plants into the woods near our house or into the garbage can, rather than into my compost pile where they would have a chance to reinfect my garden plants next season. If you have a question about what disease your plants have, there are books listed in the Bibliography which can help you find the answer.

Daily Inspection

It is worth mentioning once again that a daily visit to your garden is the best way to control both weeds and insects. You can quickly recognize changes—chewed leaves, wilted leaves, bare stems, or vanished seedlings—and take the necessary steps to remedy any problem before it has gone too far.

Watering

There is a right way and a right time to water your garden. It is fine to use the rose nozzle on your sprinkling can or hose for overhead watering in the spring and early summer, when you first plant seeds. In fact, seeds will not germinate without regular watering, and new seedlings will die very quickly if allowed to dry out. When you transplant seedlings, each one should be well watered directly in the planting hole where the roots can take a good drink to counteract the shock of transplanting. Soaking the leaves during overhead watering will often do more harm than good. A good soaking of the soil is the most efficient and effective way to water your mature vegetable plants. I leave the hose on at very low pressure, and move it from place to place letting the water trickle slowly into the soil while I am working in the garden or picking vegetables.

A good soaking is necessary only after a long dry spell, however. During the intermediate stages in your garden, a simulation of rain with your garden hose and the rose nozzle in the late afternoon is best. You should allow two or three hours of remaining daylight to dry the leaves so they do not go through the night soaking wet, which can cause mildew and fungus discases. If you can't water in the late afternoon on some days, then the early morning is next best. The early morning sun is less apt to overheat and burn wet leaves than the midday sun. In any case, you can bruise the leaves of tender plants by overhead watering with too much water pressure, and leave these plants vulnerable to disease or insects. The only time I water with high pressure in the middle of the day is when I am trying to dislodge aphids from tomatoes; but this is traumatic to the plant and should be done only as a last resort.

Overwintering

A garden bed whose soil is left completely bare all winter is apt to suffer some soil erosion from the wind and to lose nitrogen and other elements to the air. If you can count on an all-winter snow cover that is good; but if not, it is best to cover the soil with something. Undiseased plant debris is all right, but even better is to cover it with some locally available material like leaves (shredded are best), seaweed, a stable bedding of sawdust or small woodchips mixed with manure, peanut hulls, salt, or spoiled hay. If you don't have access to these materials, then a planting of winter rye seed in the late fall, but with enough time for it to grow an inch or two, will help prevent erosion and nitrogen loss. Whatever winter cover you use may be turned under in the spring to add that essential organic matter to the soil.

In conclusion I want to wish you good luck and a lot of joy as you create your garden. I hope that it will turn into a pleasantly engrossing hobby for you, as it has for me, and make you look forward to weekends at home as well as time spent in your garden each day. There are enough books to fill a lifetime of study if you want to know more about the subjects I have only touched on here. It was my intention to give you just enough to get started the right way, within the organic philosophy, because I truly believe, as Joan Gussow wrote in *The Feeding Web*, that "we must all move toward a way of living more lightly on the earth." And certainly growing your own food in the way I have described in this book is a step in that direction.

Bibliography

--------◄◉►--------

General Reference

John Jeavons. *How to Grow More Vegetables than You Ever Thought Possible on Less Land than You Can Imagine.* Berkeley, Ca.: Ten Speed Press, 1979.

Organic Gardening Editors. *Getting the Most from Your Garden.* Emmaus, Pa.: Rodale Press, Inc., 1980.

Organic Gardening. Rodale Press, Inc. Emmaus, Pa.

J. I. Rodale and staff. *How to Grow Vegetables and Fruits by the Organic Method.* Emmaus, Pa.: Rodale Press, Inc., 1961.

John Seymour. *The Self-Sufficient Gardener: A Complete Guide to Growing and Preserving All Your Own Food.* Garden City, N.Y.: Doubleday & Co., 1979.

Insect and Disease Control

Anna Carr. *Rodale's Color Handbook of Garden Insects.* Emmaus, Pa.: Rodale Press, Inc., 1979.

Helen and John Philbrick. *The Bug Book.* Charlotte, Vt.: Garden Way Publishing, 1974.

Roger B. Yepsen, Jr. *Organic Plant Protection.* Emmaus, Pa.: Rodale Press, Inc., 1976.

Soil

Lawrence D. Hills. *Fertility without Fertilizers.* New York: Universe Books, 1977.

Gene Logsdon. *The Gardener's Guide to Better Soil.* Emmaus, Pa.: Rodale Press, Inc., 1975.

Companion Planting

Joseph A. Cocannouer. *Weeds, Guardians of the Soil.* Old Greenwich, Ct.: Devin-Adair Co., n.d.

Ehrenfried E. Pfeiffer. *Weeds and What They Tell.* Springfield, Ill.: Bio-Dynamic Farming & Gardening Assoc., n.d. (Mailing address: 308 East Adams Street, Springfield, Ill., 62701.)

Helen Philbrick and Richard B. Gregg. *Companion Plants and How to Use Them.* Old Greenwich, Ct.: Devin-Adair Co., 1966.

Louise Riotte. *Secrets of Companion Planting for Successful Gardening.* Charlotte, Vt.: Garden Way Publishing, 1976.

Miscellaneous

Nancy Wilkes Bubel. *The Adventurous Gardener.* Boston: David R. Godine, 1979.

William Hytton, ed. *Rodale Herb Book: How to Use, Grow, and Buy Nature's Miracle Plants.* Emmaus, Pa.: Rodale Press, Inc., 1974.

Cookbooks

Alice Benjamin. *Cooking with Conscience.* New York: The Seabury Press, Vineyard Books, 1977.

Laurel Robertson, Carol Flinders, and Bronwen Godfrey, *Laurel's Kitchen.* Petaluma, Ca.: Nilgiri Press, 1976.

Colin Tudge. *Future Foods: Politics, Philosophy, and Recipes for the Twenty-first Century.* New York: Crown, Harmony Books, 1980.

Tools

Walter F. Nicke, Box 667G, Hudson, N.Y. 12534: Haws sprinkling can.

Smith & Hawken Tool Company, 68 Homer, Palo Alto, Ca. 94301.

Biological Controls (ladybugs, etc.)

Bo-Bio-Control, Inc., 54 South Bear Creek Drive, Merced, Ca. 95340.

World Garden Products, 2 First Street, East Norwalk, Ct., 06855.

Seed Catalogues

Burpee Seed Co., Warminster, Pa. 18974; or Clinton, Oa. 52732; or Riverside, Ca. 92502.

Burgess Seed and Plant Co., P.O. Box 3000, Galesburg, Mich. 49053.

Comstock, Ferre & Co., 263 Main Street, Wethersfield, Ct. 06109.

DeGiorgi Company, Council Bluffs, Ia. 51501 (catalogue 50¢)

Gurney Seed & Nursery Co., Yankton, S.D. 57079.

Joseph Harris Seed Company, Inc., 3670 Buffalo Road, Rochester, N.Y. 14624.

Hart Seed Company, Wethersfield, Ct. 06109.

Johnny's Selected Seeds, Albion, Me. 04910.

Meadowbrook Herb Garden, Route 138, Wyoming, R.I. 02898.

Nichols Garden Nursery, 1190 North Pacific Highway, Albany, Or. 97321.

Olds Seed Company, P.O. Box 1969, Madison, Wis. 53701.

Geo. Park Seed Co., Inc., P.O. Box 31, Greenwood, S.C. 92647.

Redwood City Seed Co., P.O. Box 361, Redwood City, Ca. 94061 (catalogue 50¢)

Reuter Seed Company, Inc., 320 N. Carrollton Ave., New Orleans, La. 70179.

R. H. Shumway, Rockford, Ill. 61101.

Stokes Seeds, Box 548, Buffalo, N.Y. 14240.

Thompson & Morgan, P.O. Box 100, Farmingdale, N.J. 07727.

Otis Twilley Seed Co., P.O. Box 65, Trevose, Pa. 19047.

Vermont Bean Seed Co., Garden Lane, Bomoseen, Vt. 05732.

Cold Frames

Rodale's Solar Growing Frame, Rodale Press, Emmaus, Pa. 18049.